MW01199511

ONE FLESH

Salvation Through Marriage in the Orthodox Church

LAWRENCE R. FARLEY

Ancient Faith Publishing • Chesterton, Indiana

One Flesh

Salvation through Marriage in the Orthodox Church

© Copyright 2013 by Lawrence R. Farley

All Rights Reserved

All Scripture quotations, unless otherwise noted, are taken from the New King James Version, © 1979, 1980, 1982 by Thomas Nelson, Inc. Used by permission.

Published by   Ancient Faith Publishing
                 A division of Ancient Faith Ministries
                 P.O. Box 748
                 Chesterton, IN 46304

Printed in the United States of America

ISBN 10: 1-936270-66-8
ISBN 13: 978-1-936270-66-8

Dedicated to my Matushka Donna,
obviously

Contents

Chapter 4

Sexuality in the Teaching of the Fathers   89

Chapter 5

The Line in the Sand   115

Chapter 6

The Meaning of the Menaion   133

Chapter 7

The Practical Conclusions   143

Introduction

Is the Church Too Negative About Sex?

MOST PEOPLE IN POPULAR CULTURE believe the Church has a distinctly negative view of sex, or at least that it retains a profound ambivalence about it. They believe the Church, in its secret heart of hearts, thinks that sex was not, after all, one of God's better ideas, and therefore should be avoided as much as possible.

This is reflected in a quip of Dorothy L. Sayers, Christian apologist and writer of detective fiction. She once wrote, "A young man once said to me with perfect simplicity, 'I did not know there were seven deadly sins; please tell me the names of the other six'" (from her essay "The Other Six Deadly Sins"). Miss Sayers was commenting on the world's belief that as far as the Church is concerned, deadly sin equals sexual sin, as if sexual sin were the Church's chief preoccupation. Popular culture thinks that, for the Church, all sin has somehow coalesced into the single sin of lust, and that is why Christians are so negative about sex.

This is nonsense, of course, but one does see how people might come up with this idea. Sayers again writes in the same essay, "Do the officials stationed at church doors in Italy to exclude women with bare arms turn anybody away on the grounds that they are too well dressed to be honest?" We Christians often do give the impression that sexual sins are the worst ones, so that we focus more on mildly immodest clothing, suggesting possible sexual immorality, than rich clothing, suggesting wealth acquired through possibly dishonest business practices.

Indeed, "immorality" is often read as "sexual immorality," when in fact it is possible to be immoral in all sorts of different ways. Sayers again: "A man may be greedy and selfish; spiteful, cruel, jealous, and unjust; violent and brutal; grasping, unscrupulous, and a liar; stubborn and arrogant, stupid, morose and dead to every noble instinct—and still we are ready to say of him that he is not an immoral man."

Sayers is accurately taking the pulse of our popular culture—taught by generations of Christian moralists, the world says that "immorality" equals "sexual immorality." Even the New American Standard translation of the Bible is not immune from this false equation: when St. Paul writes in 1 Corinthians 6:18 that we should "flee fornication" (Gr. *porneia*), the NASB translates it, "Flee immorality." The world can be forgiven for thinking that Christians equate real sin with sexual sin because of a fundamental Christian ambivalence about sex.

Traveling from the ecclesiastical West to the East does not improve matters much in the popular mind. Orthodoxy does indeed demand of its faithful that as their preparation for receiving Holy Communion, they fast not only from food but also from sexual activity. And not just on Saturday nights, preparing to receive the Eucharist on Sunday morning—such sexual abstinence is counseled during the fasting periods of the church year as well, which some have calculated as comprising about a third of the entire year. Insistence on such abstinence gives the impression that the Church is rather down on sex.

And then there is the matter of monasticism. We Orthodox reserve a warm appreciation for monks and nuns, admiring them for their sanctity and holding them up for our spiritual applause. This is not wrong, but it does nothing to promote our assertion that we are not, after all, too negative about sex.

If we are *not* negative about sex, the world asks, then why are our big heroes all celibates? And that includes the upper levels of church leadership, for the church insists that all its bishops be monks. This demand for an unmarried clergy even extends to the parish priest in some ways, for if the wife of a married parish priest dies, that priest is not allowed canonically to remarry, and if he does, he is to be deposed. It is as if the Church says to its clergy, "We will grudgingly allow you to marry, O priest, but only once."

This seems to be confirmed in the Church's choice of those it glorifies as saints, for once again, celibates seem to predominate. Even a book extolling married saints focuses on saints who, though once married, later chose celibacy, as if marriage and sexuality were at best the unfortunate introduction to the life of real sanctity, which of course consisted of celibacy. (To take one example among many, St. John of Kronstadt, though married, refused to have sex with his wife, insisting over her initial protests that they live together as brother and sister.)

In this book on married saints, attention is given to saints who either chose to combine lawful marriage with celibacy, or were once sexually active with their wives, but when they became serious about holiness of course they gave up being sexually active to embrace celibacy, which was hailed as "the angelic life." The world asks: If celibates are "angelic," what does this say about those who are not celibate but continue to be sexually active with their spouses within lawful marriage? What is the opposite or alternative to being angelic? One begins to see how the world might get the idea that the Church retains a rather dim view of sex.

The Church has long been perceived to have either a negative attitude toward sexuality or at best a profoundly ambivalent one. But is this perception an accurate one? Let us examine the theme of sexuality in the life of the Christian and how we should deal with the fact that God has made us gendered beings. We begin where the Apostles and the Fathers would begin—by examining the Scriptures.

Chapter 1

Sexuality in the Old Testament

FOR A CHRISTIAN, any discussion of sexuality must begin in Genesis, with the creation stories, for these contain the first and most fundamental statement of human sexuality in the Scriptures. There, in Genesis 1:26–31, we read the following:

> Then God said, "Let Us make man [Heb. *adam*] in Our image, according to Our likeness; let them have dominion over the fish of the sea, over the birds of the air, and over the cattle, over all the earth and over every creeping thing that creeps on the earth." So God created man [Heb. *adam*] in His *own* image; in the image of God He created him; male and female He created them. Then God blessed them, and God said to them, "Be fruitful and multiply; fill the earth and subdue it; have dominion over the fish of the sea, over the birds of the air, and over every living thing that moves on the earth." . . . God saw everything that He had made, and indeed *it was* very good.

To this first account of the creation of man and woman is added a second account, in Genesis 2:18–25:

> And the LORD God said, "*It is* not good that man [Heb. *adam*] should be alone; I will make him a helper comparable to him." Out of the ground the LORD God formed every beast of the field and every bird of the air, and brought *them* to Adam ["the man"] to see what he would call them. And whatever Adam called each living creature, that *was* its name. So Adam gave names to all cattle, to the birds of the air, and to every beast of the field. But for Adam there was not found a helper comparable to him. And the LORD God caused a deep sleep to fall on Adam, and he slept; and He took one of his ribs, and closed up the flesh in its place. Then the rib which the LORD God had taken from man [Heb. *adam*] He made into a woman [Heb. *ishah*], and He brought her to the man. And Adam said,
>
> > "This *is* now bone of my bones,
> > And flesh of my flesh;
> > She shall be called Woman [Heb. *ishah*],
> > Because she was taken out of Man [Heb. *ish*]."
>
> Therefore a man [Heb. *ish*] shall leave his father and mother and be joined to his wife, and they shall become one flesh. And they were both naked, the man [Heb. *adam*] and his wife [Heb. *ishah*], and were not ashamed.

To these stories must also be added the story of the Fall. We focus in particular on the curses that fall upon the man and the woman, as found in Genesis 3:16–19:

> To the woman [Heb. *ishah*] He said:
> "I will greatly multiply your sorrow and your conception;

In pain you shall bring forth children;
Your desire *shall be* for your husband,
And he shall rule over you."

Then to Adam He said, "Because you have heeded the voice of your wife [Heb. *ishah*], and have eaten from the tree of which I commanded you, saying, 'You shall not eat of it':

"Cursed *is* the ground for your sake;
In toil you shall eat *of* it
All the days of your life.
Both thorns and thistles it shall bring forth for you,
And you shall eat the herb of the field.
In the sweat of your face you shall eat bread
Till you return to the ground [Heb. *adamah*],
For out of it you were taken;
For dust you *are,*
And to dust you shall return."

In these scriptural citations, we have preserved some of the original Hebrew, so that we can more easily recognize that "adam" is not so much a personal name (like "Joseph" or "Ken") as it is a designation; we are speaking not just about the fate of two individuals, but about the story of humanity, about Man and Woman.

Though of course a full exegesis of these stories is beyond the scope of the present work, a few observations may be made about them. We make these observations recognizing that the Genesis creation story is not primarily about sexuality, or even about human origins, but about the power of the Jewish God. Its fundamental message is not, "This is how the world began" (no ancient cared much about that), but rather, "The tribal God of the Hebrews is the one true God, sovereign over all the earth—and therefore able to protect His people." Nonetheless, certain conclusions about human sexuality may legitimately be drawn.

First of all, we note from the first creation story in Genesis 1:26–31 that the human species (Heb. *adam*) is bipartite. In this first creation account, *adam* consists of both male and female. For when the story says that God made *adam*/humanity "in His image," the text goes on to state, "male and female He created them." *Adam*, the human person, is a gendered being. Thus it was not the case that God made the male in His image and added the female later as an afterthought, an additional enhancement, like adding air-conditioning to a basic car—sexuality and sexual differentiation is portrayed as essential to humanity.

We can also see the importance of gender when we consider the nature of the divine image (Heb. *tselem*), which both male and female share. What is this "image"? Many writers have written about this, some supposing the image was the rational part of humanity or the human capacity for free choice. These observations are not wrong and are legitimate deductions, but the text says something else. In particular it connects the image of God with the authority of God—that is, *adam* exercises the authority of God on earth as His regent, as His image.

In other passages of the Old Testament, the word *tselem* is used for images and statues of the pagan gods (e.g. Num. 33:52). The thought of these passages is that the pagan god is somehow present through its image or statue. In the same way, *adam* functions as the image of God—God's authority is present on earth through His *adam*. To be God's "image" is to function as His regent. That is why immediately after saying that "God created *adam* in His *own image*" (Gen. 1:27), the text goes on to say, "God said to them, "Be fruitful and multiply; fill the earth and subdue it; *have dominion . . . over every living thing that moves on the earth*" (v. 28, emphasis added). It is as God's *tselem* that the man and woman rule.

Note that this "dominion" presupposes not just a shared activity (both male and female rule together), but also sexual activity—for they rule the earth by being "fruitful" and by "multiplying." That is how they "fill the earth and subdue it." Put plainly, the man and woman fulfill their role as God's *tselem* on earth by having sex and having babies.

We see this also in the preamble to this verse: "God blessed them." God's "blessing" consists of the bestowal of fecundity (which is how the verb is usually used in the Hebrew Scriptures). We nowadays use the term "bless" very generally; in many Orthodox circles, "to bless" often means simply "to grant permission." That is fine, but it is not the basic use of the term in the Old Testament. There "to bless" means to give life, virility, fertility: when God "blesses" a man, his wife is "like a fruitful vine," his children "like olive plants" (i.e., numerous) around his table (Ps. 128:1-3). The sign that "the people whose God *is* the Lord" are blessed is that they have sons and daughters, their garners are full, their flocks bring forth thousands and ten thousands, and their cattle bear without mishap (Ps. 144:12-15). In the New Testament, blessing is spiritualized, but this advance should not make us miss the fact that in the Genesis narratives and the Old Testament generally, blessing involves fecundity and multiplying—in other words, sex.

The second creation story, in Genesis 2:18-25, focuses on the creation of woman. If in the first creation story Man and Woman are created together, after all the world was made, to rule over that world as God's image, in this second story we have a narrower and more precise focus. That is, woman is considered in her relation to man. Once again, a complete exegesis of the passage is beyond the scope of this book, but a few observations may be made.

First of all, the creation of woman is necessary for the goodness of creation. In the first story (Gen. 1:31) we read that everything God created was "very good" (Heb. *tov*). In the second story, we read about a situation when it was not yet "very good"—indeed, God pronounced after the creation of the *adam* that it was not good (Heb. *tov*) for him to be alone. For man's situation to become *tov*, God must make him a helper "comparable to him." The word here is the Hebrew *kenegdo*, literally, "as in front of him," face to face, a counterpart to him.

The creation of the animals in this story is part of a plan to find a helper that corresponds to the *adam*. No animal can fill this role; none can serve as a true counterpart. (One imagines this creation and parade of animals before Man was not a matter of God conducting a series of unsuccessful experiments so much as educating Man about his true need.)

At last, all other options exhausted, God causes a deep sleep to fall upon the man, for he would have no active part in what God was about to do. God took one of the man's "ribs" (Heb. *tsela*, "a side"; it is the word used for one of the sides of the ark of the covenant in Ex. 25:12), and used this part of the *adam's* very and inmost self to fashion into a woman, a true counterpart for man.

When God brought His new creation to the *adam*, the man

exclaimed, "This is now bone of my bones and flesh of my flesh!" It was a cry of delight, a recognition that this at last was the long-sought counterpart, the one that could complete him so that things were now *tov*, as God first intended. As he named the rest of creation (Gen. 2:19–20), so he names this creation also, and the name he bestows is significant. She is *ishah*, for she was taken out of *ish*. The word *ish* is the Hebrew for "man" in the sense of "male person"; "-*ah*" is the feminine ending to a noun. Thus the new creation is a feminine *adam*, a feminine *ish*. That is, she was his true self.

"Therefore" (the text goes on to say), a man (Heb. *ish*) in the society that would later arise would "leave his father and mother," severing the most intimate and sacred of ties, in order to be "joined to his wife, and they shall become one flesh" (Gen. 2:24). The bond between the *adam* and his *ishah* was so wonderful, perfect, and divinely given that it would even supersede the sacred bonds of family (sacred bonds indeed in the ancient Near East). Gender differentiation and sexuality are not just "very good" (Gen. 1:31); without them, the goodness of the human situation/divine creation would be lacking. Not only is sexuality not evil or compromised; it is essential to the goodness God intended.

We also see in this story how gender, with its combination of identity and difference (the *ishah* is the same as the *ish*, but different and feminized), is a source of delight to the man. In the Hebrew text, things of lasting and fundamental import are often presented in poetry, not prose. Thus, for example, after the Fall, God's sentences upon the serpent, the woman, and the man are given as poetry (Gen. 3:14f). Thus God's promise of the stability of creation after the Flood is given as poetry (Gen. 8:22). Here we see that the *adam's* spontaneous cry when he first sees the woman is given in poetry. This does not merely indicate the fundamental nature of the creation of gender, but also the intensity of the *adam's* joy. The first poem in history (as far as the biblical text is concerned) is a love poem. This witnesses to the essential joyfulness of gender. The goodness of sex is summarized in the final word of the story: "And they were both naked, the man [Heb. *adam*] and his wife [Heb. *ishah*], and were not ashamed."

We conclude our examination by looking briefly at parts of the story of the Fall (Gen. 3:16f). Many writers have concluded that although sexuality was innocent "in the Garden," before the Fall, the Fall introduced a change in sexuality so fundamental and far-reaching that it could no longer be considered *tov,* or good. The Fall changed everything, including the goodness of sexuality.

Many writers have presumed this. St. Augustine, that prolific preacher and writer whose works have so influenced Western Catholic Christianity, taught that sex was unfallen while Adam and Eve were still in the Garden, and if they had never fallen, sex would have continued in its original blissful, unfallen state; but after the Fall, even married sexuality is tainted with some degree of sinfulness.

Some Eastern Fathers suggested that sex was created by God only because He foreknew that Adam and Eve would fall and die, and therefore be in need of some mode of reproduction to save the human species from extinction. For these writers, an unfallen world would need no sex and have no room for it. For them, sex is definitely "Plan B"—a conclusion they drew from our Lord's words about there being no marrying and giving in marriage in the resurrection and the age to come (Matt. 22:30). For them, the age to come represents a return to the bliss originally intended before the Fall, and since in the age to come men and women will not marry or be sexually active, but will be like the genderless "angels in heaven," then such an asexual state must have been the original ideal. Divine foreknowledge of the Fall, they suggest, meant that this ideal was not put into effect in the first creation, but will be in the age to come when God's original purposes are finally fulfilled.

We will examine the Fathers later. Here we only note that the sentences passed by God on the *adam* and his wife contain no hint of a change regarding sexuality. Both the man and the woman must continue to fulfill their divinely given tasks: man must till the soil (his natural ecological partner, since *adam* was first created from the *adamah*, the soil; Gen. 2:9), and woman must give birth to offspring as the natural result of being one flesh with the man. But now the sentence of death, of mortality, grief, and sorrow, overshadows all.

The sentence of death ("in the day that you eat of [the tree] you shall surely die"; Gen. 2:17) means that the man must do his work "in toil." His natural ecological partner, the *adamah*, or soil, will no longer joyfully give up its fruit. It will produce thorns and thistles for the man, so that the man will eat his bread (i.e., live) "in the sweat of [his] face" (Gen. 3:17–19). The sentence of death brings the same changes for the woman also: she must do her work of childbearing now "in pain." What was originally meant as purely joyful and easy work is now a work of pain and weakness (Gen. 3:16).

Some have suggested that the element of sexual desire is introduced for the first time in God's sentence on the woman in verse 16: "your desire *shall be* for your husband," and they further suggest that the authority of husband over wife is first introduced here as well: "and he shall rule over you." This would indeed cast a profound shadow over the scriptural portrayal of sexuality, for it would mean that sexual desire itself is fallen. Is this what this text means?

We can speak plainly regarding the second suggestion—that the authority of the husband is introduced here for the first time with the words "he shall rule over you." This cannot be the introduction of such subordination, because the subordination was clearly presented earlier, when the *adam* named his wife. Naming in the ancient Near East was a function of authority, and the naming of the animals by the *adam* showed his authority over them. Similarly, his naming of the newly created woman showed and established his authority over her as well. The "ruling" of Genesis 3:16 cannot therefore refer to the original subordination of the *ishah* to her *ish*. To what then does it refer?

I would suggest that it refers to her weakened state. The sentence of death given to the man is manifested in his weakness: the soil, once subject to him, now must be toiled over ceaselessly and will only reluctantly yield its fruit, along with thorns and thistles. The man, once strong and in control, is now reduced to painful labor.

The same situation applies to the woman. In her weakness, her desire will be for her husband—that is, she will need his protection, his shelter. It is in this sense that he will "rule" over her.

That is, just as the sun "rules over" the day (Heb. *mashal*) as giver of light and life, so now the man must rule over (Heb. *mashal*) his wife also. The woman's "desire" for her husband is her turning to him in reliance for protection in her weakness. This appears to be the view of the Septuagint translator as well, who translated the text, "your recourse [Gr. *apostrophe*] shall be to your husband." This passage therefore has nothing to do with sexual desire, but only with the desire for protection of someone vulnerable and weakened.

Overall, we see in the creation stories a remarkably positive view of sexuality. It was created by God and was essential to the goodness of His creation. It was an integral part of humanity's being made in the image of God. And there is nothing in the narrative to suggest that the Fall affected its essential goodness.

The Patriarchal Narratives and the Law

In the stories about the patriarchs, one of the main concerns is procreation. This is not surprising, given that God promised to Abraham and Sarah descendants like the stars in heaven for multitude and as numerous as the sand on the seashore (Gen. 22:17), despite the fact that Abraham was an old man and Sarah well past the years of childbearing. As a gift from God, Sarah would receive the miraculous ability to conceive Abraham's son, and from this son Isaac others would be born in such numbers as to fill the Promised Land.

In this context, the emphasis was on the mere fact of procreation, not the love a husband might have for his wife. This was consistent with marriage in the culture of that time: marriage was not based on romance or the romantic choices of those involved. It was primarily an economic arrangement, set up by the parents of those being married for reasons of economic advantage and family alliances. This flies in the face of contemporary approaches, where the romantic love and individual choice of those being married are paramount; but it was simply the norm in the ancient world.

This rather prosaic approach to marriage continued to be reflected in the Mosaic Law, where marriage was a match arranged by the parents of the bride and groom for the economic advantage and security of each. The provisions of the Law accordingly are concerned with the externals and legalities of such matches—with such things as using some compassion when taking a wife from enemies defeated in battle (Deut. 21:10f), or divorcing a wife found to be previously unchaste (Deut. 22:13f), or handling serial divorces (Deut. 24:1f). The Mosaic Law was primarily a legal code governing the total life of a people in transition from a nomadic life to a settled one, a life and culture in which family honor was paramount. The family, not the state, was the primary focus of one's day-to-day existence, and so the laws are concerned with reinforcing the stability of the family.

Yet even so, what we would today term emotional attachment could not be altogether avoided. We see such emotional attachments (darkened by obsession and lust) in Hamor's attraction to and rape of Dinah in Genesis 34, in David's attraction to and adultery with Bathsheba in 2 Samuel 11, and in Amnon's attraction to and rape of his sister Tamar in 2 Samuel 13.

Happily, the Scriptures also report numerous examples of healthy and less tragic emotional attachments. Thus we read in passing that in the choice of Rebekah as a wife for Isaac, not only did economics play a role (Abraham's servant sent to find a wife for Isaac brought out "jewelry of silver, jewelry of gold, and clothing, and gave *them* to Rebekah" as gifts; Gen. 24:53), but beauty as well—for the text relates that "the young woman *was* very beautiful" (Gen. 24:16). In his mature years Isaac could still enjoy the presence of Rebekah his bride. Though he told those in Gerar that Rebekah was his sister (something of a family tradition to ensure safety; compare Gen. 12:13; 20:2), he was found out because people saw him caressing her in public (Gen. 26:8).

Also, Jacob, staying with his relative Laban and working for him, was quite taken with his daughter Rachel and was willing to work for Laban for seven years to win her. Even when he was deceived by Laban and married off to his daughter Leah instead (quite a surprise the morning after!), he was willing to work for another seven years for Rachel. And yet the text records that this time "seemed to him but a few days because of his love for her" (Gen. 29:20).

Clearly romantic love is not simply a modern invention. We may even see such things written between the lines of the Mosaic Law: in Deuteronomy 21:15f we find the case of a man who had two wives, "one loved and the other unloved." This law stipulates that the man may not prefer the son of the loved wife above that of the unloved wife if the latter is the firstborn. The point is that even in a culture in which polygamy was tolerated, a man might prefer one wife over the other—a sticky situation to be sure and not ideal, but one that nonetheless witnesses indirectly to what we would term a romantic attachment to one woman over the other. Even in such cultures as those reflected in the Mosaic Law, with their practical and prosaic approach to marriage, the voice of the human heart could not be completely silenced.

The Admonitions of the Book of Proverbs

In the days when marriage was the fundamental building block of society and when family was the usual and often final court of appeal for justice, society's main concern was to preserve the stability of marriage. Accordingly, the wisdom literature of the Old Testament, such as the Book of Proverbs, is replete with warnings against adultery. It warns against the attractions and wiles of the "strange woman"—or as we would say, the exotic woman, all the more attractively seductive for her foreignness (see, for example, Prov. 2:16f; 5:1f).

It is significant what Proverbs offers as an alternative and incentive to avoid such sin. It is true that it provides warnings against disease (5:11), public disgrace (5:14), and financial ruin (6:32f) as consequences that should warn one off from the sin of infidelity. But in addition to these negative inducements to righteousness and marital faithfulness, it provides a positive one as well, and one worth quoting at length. In Proverbs 5:15–19 we read:

> Drink water from your own cistern,
> And running water from your own well.
> Should your fountains be dispersed abroad,
> Streams of water in the streets?

Let them be only your own,
And not for strangers with you.
Let your fountain be blessed,
And rejoice with the wife of your youth.
As a loving deer and a graceful doe,
Let her breasts satisfy you at all times;
And always be enraptured with her love.

The passage is remarkable and almost modern in its frankness, and is read in the Orthodox Church at one of the Lenten Liturgies of the Presanctified Gifts. Some translators have apparently felt the text is a bit too frank and have altered the literal translation somewhat. Where the Hebrew reads, "let her breasts (Heb. *dadim*, compare use in Ezek. 23:3) satiate you (Heb. *ravah*, compare use in Prov. 7:18) at all times," other translations opt for more demure readings. The RSV translates it as "let her affection fill you at all times with delight"; the New English Bible reads, "her love will continually wrap you around." The Good News Bible reads (with touching unintentional archaism) "let her charms keep you happy."

Perhaps most different of all is that of the Orthodox Study Bible, which faithfully reflects the straitlaced Septuagint. It reads, "Let her alone go before you and be with you at all times, for in living with her love, you will be great"—which has all the feel of an edifying sermon, even if it is at the cost of reproducing what the original actually says. The fact is that the original exults in the sensuality of married love, offering that sensuality as an alternative to the dark and forbidden temptations of adultery with "the strange woman." While some may think it an odd choice for

Lenten liturgical reading, it is an important note to be sounded in the Hebrew canon of Scripture, for it reveals that sexual desire finds its natural, safe, and spiritually useful home within marriage.

The Song of Solomon

No survey of the Old Testament material on sexuality would be complete without reference to the Song of Solomon, sometimes called "the Song of Songs." Its inclusion (late) within the Hebrew canon is in many ways remarkable, for there is almost no reference to God, prayer, or spirituality within the text. Even the Book of Tobit offered the usual pious advice about marriage in the form of the religious example of mutual prayer on the wedding night (Tobit 8:4f: "Sister," (says the groom), "get up and let us pray that the Lord may have mercy upon us").

But the Song of Solomon offers no such "spiritual" component, no sop to piety, no suggestion that its sensuality needed to be justified by religious piety. In fact, piety does not enter into it at all—any more than it does to the original and authentic text of the Book of Esther. In the original of Esther, no prayers are recorded, despite all the protagonists' trust in God and the crisis of their time. When Mordecai heard of the decree against the Jews, he rent his clothes, put on sackcloth, and wailed, but no prayer is recorded or even referred to. Later religious writers found such omissions too intolerably secular and took pains to add to the original (in the form of a prayer after Esther 4:17 they felt sure Mordecai would have prayed).

The Song of Solomon is at least as "secular" as the original of

Esther, but it is so relentlessly sensual that such writers as added to Esther could apparently find no way to "spiritualize" the Song of Solomon. Thus it remains an erotic love poem throughout, with no hint of "spirituality."

Pious souls have long felt this to be a problem. Take, for example, Rabbi Akiva, who lived at the end of the first century and the beginning of the second. People were wont to sing rather explicit songs at weddings, no doubt praising the bride and the groom for their attributes. Some people apparently used the text of the Song of Solomon for this end, and Rabbi Akiva was incensed. Such people, he fumed and fulminated, have no share in eternal life in the age to come. Then as now, many consider the material in this biblical book rather too explicit.

It is indeed an overwhelming book, especially when read in one sitting. Its structure and format are far from clear. Is there an overarching plot, a development in the relationship of the man and the woman (thought by many to be Solomon and his love)? Is it one continuous song or a collection of many songs? Opinions vary, and a quick perusal of a seminary's library bookshelf will reveal as many views as there are commentators. What is beyond dispute is the unceasing barrage of sensuality, of joyful delight in the physical attraction between the lovers.

The book begins with an exclamation: "Let him kiss me with the kisses of his mouth!"—that is, with deep kisses, not just the kisses of the lips. Such passion sets the tone for the book. The book consists of a dialogue between the man and the woman, each praising the other with a wealth of sexual imagery. All the senses are appealed to—hearing (Songs 2:14; 5:2), taste (2:3, 5; 3:2; 4:11;

5:1), touch (2:6; 5:2), and especially (adding to the eroticism of the poem) smell (1:3, 12–13; 2:13; 3:6; 4:6, 10–11, 14, 16; 5:5, 13; 7:13; 8:14).

Of course, most of the Song is given over to the delights of sight, and we find long passages in which the lovers describe one another in precise detail, the man starting at the top of the woman and working his way down (4:1–6) and the woman doing the same for the man (5:10–16). References to flowers and fruit and spices abound in the text. So also do double entendres. To quote but one of them, in 2:17 the woman invites her lover to "turn, my beloved, and be like a gazelle or a young stag on the mountains of Bether." Bether? A marginal note reads "or, cleavage." The overall impression of the book is quite overwhelming. The Song is a hymn of praise, a duet sung by two lovers to each other, the words of lovers utterly captivated by each other.

In this song, we see the ultimate meaning of the original plan of God in creation in making two persons into "one flesh," for in this song there is no room for another. The two lovers look relentlessly and unceasingly at each other, with no possibility of a third coming between them. In this vision, the very possibility of polygamy (or, come to that, of divorce) is utterly excluded: the man cleaves to his beloved so deeply that he could have no desire or thought of another woman and no consideration of possibly one day ending the relationship. Given the historical context of Solomon (with his seven hundred wives and three hundred concubines; 1 Kin. 11:3), such commitment to eternal and enthusiastic monogamy is all the more impressive. The Song of Solomon is not royal autobiography; it is visionary idealism—the fulfillment of the idealism established originally by God when He made the man and the woman to become "one flesh."

The Fathers were happy to mine this book for spiritual gold. Gregory of Nyssa, for example, wrote a famous commentary on it, treating the book as an allegory of the soul's love for God. We see the survival of such use in the headings over the pages in some Bibles: in one old King James Bible, for example, the topic heading over one page (the page containing 4:5) reads, "The church glorieth in Christ."

Such approaches are not wrong, since all human love is rooted in the divine love. Even St. Paul declared that marriage is a hidden revelation, a *mysterion* of the love Christ has for His Church (Eph. 5:32). But it is important also not to miss the significance of the inclusion of this book in the Hebrew canon of Scripture, for before the Song of Solomon is theology, it is erotic love poetry. This means that the God by whose providence such a work was included in the list of sacred Scripture is a God who delights in sexual love—at least in the sexual love between those as deeply committed to one another as were those whose words were recorded in the Song, a love and commitment to the other which is "as strong as death" (8:6). With the Song of Songs we reach the zenith of praise for sexual love, and its inclusion as Holy Writ means that God considers the sexuality He made to be "very *tov*."

Summary of the Old Testament Teaching

The Old Testament is a collection of ancient documents, and therefore it mirrors to some degree the culture of its day. But it does include some surprises, and the teaching in the Old Testament is more startling and revolutionary than some might expect. Like any ancient document, it considers marriage primarily as an economic union, one that provides the foundation for society and for the safety of its members. Thus marriage has its prosaic aspect, with sexuality functioning to satisfy human needs and appetites and for the procreation of children. But the revolutionary teaching in the creation stories carries through as well, like leaven leavening the lump, and providing for perhaps some surprising results.

In the ancient Near East, women were essentially chattel, which allowed for easy divorce and for polygamy. The creation stories run counter to this and contradict it. In these stories, a woman is not chattel, but shares with the husband the rule of God over the earth as his co-equal fellow-ruler. She also is made in the image of God (an image reserved for kings in the culture of that day). She is his ontological equal, an *ishah* corresponding in every way and completing the *ish*, bone of his bones and flesh of his flesh.

Such correspondence and equality allows for the possibility of transfiguring what would otherwise be a simple economic union. The natural affection between man and wife can be transformed into something more—man and wife can become Lover and Beloved, delighting in each other *as persons*. Normal marital affection can blossom into the delight glimpsed in Proverbs 5:15f and celebrated uproariously throughout the Song of Solomon. The original surprise and joy with which the first man greeted the first woman can take root in all the marriages that follow.

Sexuality can become the vehicle for expressing this delight and for appreciating the other as God's gift. It therefore becomes not simply an appetite that results in procreation, but potentially a way of self-transcendence, of receiving a joy that takes one out of oneself and roots one's joy in another. In other words, even in the Old Testament, sexuality can become the beginning of sanctification.

Chapter 2

Old Things in the New Testament

THE NEW TESTAMENT REPRESENTS an advance over the Old Testament, for on the one hand it reproduces and intensifies its teaching, and on the other hand introduces truths scarcely dreamt of by those who lived before Christ. The Lord Jesus Himself says this when He says that a scribe who had been "instructed concerning the Kingdom of Heaven" (that is, a scribe who had become His disciple) was "like a householder who brings out of his treasure things new and old" (Matt. 13:52). In our Lord's day, a family's storerooms were stocked with all sorts of things, new and old, and a wise head of the family would provide out of that storeroom whatever was needed. In the same way, our Lord says, a Jewish scribe who had become His disciple would find some of the things he had learned confirmed by Him and would also receive truths never before dreamt of. The scribe had to keep his heart and mind open to new things.

The New Testament therefore confirms certain things taught

by the Law and the Prophets, cutting to the heart of them and even intensifying their force. It also introduces other things a Jew would consider unheard-of and revolutionary, thus challenging us to keep up with the God who does "new things" (Is. 43:19). A Christian scribe or teacher therefore will look at treasures "new and old." In this chapter we will examine some of the "old things," teachings consistent with what has already been given us in the Law and the Prophets.

Avoiding Fornication

In Israel, among Jews, the Church could take for granted that those who chose to accept baptism and become disciples of Jesus would avoid fornication, for any pious Jew would avoid it, being taught by such things as the commandment "You shall not commit adultery" (Ex. 20:14) and the material we have alluded to in the Book of Proverbs.

When the Church moved out into pagan territory among the Gentiles, however, such behavior could not be taken for granted. In the pagan world, fornication (for men) was accepted as normal. Indeed, one gets the idea that the average pagan man could make little sense out of the Church's insistence on sexual purity and avoiding fornication. That is doubtless why the prohibition was given so repeatedly in the apostolic writings.

Take, for example, one of the earliest of Paul's letters, First Thessalonians. To these new Gentile converts he wrote:

> Finally then, brethren, we urge and exhort in the Lord Jesus that
> you should abound more and more, just as you received from us

how you ought to walk and to please God; for you know what commandments we gave you through the Lord Jesus. For this is the will of God, your sanctification: that you should abstain from sexual immorality[Gr. *porneia*]; that each of you should know how to possess his own vessel in sanctification and honor, not in passion of lust, like the Gentiles who do not know God. (1 Thess. 4:1–5)

Note that Paul speaks of the change of behavior required by the Gospel first in terms of avoiding fornication, as if this were the most important thing. In fact, he refers to "the will of God" for them entirely in terms of avoiding this sexual sin. He has no other ethical counsel to offer them in this section, except to add secondarily (having secured a commitment to sexual purity) that they must love one another, living lives of quiet industry (1 Thess. 4:9–12).

However, it would be a mistake to assume from this passage that the morality and changed life demanded by Christian discipleship consist primarily in avoiding fornication, as if fornication were the worst sin and the only one worth warning against. Paul was not writing a compendium of moral theology; he was giving urgently needed guidance to raw, newly converted pagans. Later on, in the months and years to come, the "meat" of other teaching would be offered, but to begin with, these new baby Christians needed the "milk" of the ethical basics (compare Heb. 5:12–14). Paul describes their "sanctification" as abstaining from fornication because this was the most prominent difference in their new life, the thing that most differed from their old ways, and this change could not be taken for granted.

We note also this insistence on avoiding fornication in the text of the circular letter written by the first apostolic council in Jerusalem in about AD 49 and found in Acts 15:23-29. This gathering was called to deal with a crisis and division in the Church—namely the vexed question of whether new Gentile converts needed to become circumcised in order to continue to be disciples of the Jewish Messiah and worshippers of the Jewish God. Paul's opponents answered, "Yes, these Gentiles did need to be circumcised" (i.e., they had to become Jewish to fully worship the Jewish God), while Paul himself answered, "No, they didn't need to be circumcised, but were fully acceptable to God as disciples of Jesus while remaining Gentiles."

A council met in Jerusalem at which the apostles and elders of the Mother Church would decide this question. They decided in favor of the latter position, thus vindicating Paul's mission to the Gentiles. Part of the letter they sent to be read to the churches affected by their verdict read as follows: "For it seemed good to the Holy Spirit, and to us, to lay upon you no greater burden than these necessary things: that you abstain from things offered to idols, from blood, from things strangled, and from sexual immorality. If you keep yourselves from these, you will do well" (Acts 15:28-29).

The first thing to notice in this list of essentials is that circumcision is not among them. The Gentiles were not required to become Jewish, but could remain uncircumcised Gentiles and still remain fully communicant disciples of Christ. All the council insisted on was that they abide by the so-called "Covenant of

Noah"—that is, laws incumbent upon all men, mentioned in Genesis 9 after Noah's Flood. These few laws formed in Jewish eyes the basic foundation of all human morality.

The covenant included a prohibition against eating blood and assumed the avoidance of idolatry. Consistent with this, the apostolic council required that new Gentile converts to Christ also avoid "blood" (i.e., eating blood), "things strangled" (i.e., eating things with the blood left in them), and "things offered to idols" (i.e., participating in idolatry). And at the end of the list of prohibited behaviors, we find "sexual immorality" (Gr. *porneia*, lit. "fornication"). Although fornication was not found in the material in Genesis 9, the apostles considered the behavior to be too much an ingrained part of Gentile life to be left out of the list of prohibitions. Accordingly, it also finds a place on the list of things from which new converts must abstain.

Possibly in no other pagan city was fornication more normalized than in Corinth—indeed, the debauchery of Corinth was proverbial and famous, so that the city gave its name to a verb. "To Corinthianize" meant to go on a drunken and lustful debauch. The city was home to the temple of Aphrodite, to which many priestesses were attached as sacred prostitutes, and in the evening they descended from the Acropolis to offer their services on the streets of the city. In Corinth, therefore, fornication was something of a civic tradition, and converts to the Christian Faith there needed to be told that this civic tradition had no place in the apostolic traditions of the Church.

Thus it was that St. Paul wrote to the Corinthians that they must shun fornication, and he strove to provide them with a convincing rationale. His words in 1 Corinthians 6:13-20 are worth quoting in full:

> Now the body *is* not for sexual immorality but for the Lord, and the Lord for the body. And God both raised up the Lord and will also raise us up by His power. Do you not know that your bodies are members of Christ? Shall I then take the members of Christ and make *them* members of a harlot? Certainly not! Or do you not know that he who is joined to a harlot is one body *with her?* For "the two," He says, "shall become one flesh." But he who is joined to the Lord is one spirit *with Him.* Flee sexual immorality. Every sin that a man does is outside the body, but he who commits sexual immorality sins against his own body. Or do you not know that your body is the temple of the Holy Spirit *who is* in you, whom you have from God, and you are not your own? For you were bought at a price; therefore glorify God in your body and in your spirit, which are God's.

In this passage, St. Paul grounds the prohibition against fornication in the nature of the act itself—namely that it creates a lasting union with the person with whom one shares his or her body. Like a good Jew, he refers for proof to the Scriptures, in this case the original creation story. In this story, the first created man is joined to his wife, with the result that the two persons become "one flesh"—or, as we might say, a single organism. That is, they now belong together as a single whole and cannot be separated, any more than a single organism can be safely torn in half.

This deep unity that makes the two into one is not the result of promises exchanged between the two, or of commitment between them, or of any romantic attachment between them. It results solely from the sexual act itself, even if there is no commitment between the two partners. The unity of being one flesh occurs whether or not the two sexual partners want it to occur—for Paul says such a union occurs between a man and a paid prostitute, between whom there is presumably no intention of lasting commitment or even of repeated acquaintance. Nonetheless, their shared sexual experience results in their becoming one flesh.

This is the problem with fornication for the Christian: It establishes a union between the believer and someone else with whom the believer cannot properly make such a union. The believer is already a member or a part of Christ, having been joined to Him in baptism so that he is now "one spirit" with Him, sharing life with Him on the deepest level. Such a person is not free to be joined to another such as a prostitute, for that would be to mix the holiness of the Lord with the unholiness of the prostitute.

It is in this sense that "he who commits sexual immorality sins against his own body," for he violates the deepest part of himself. Other sins, of course, are wrong too. The believer should also avoid the sin of theft, the sin of murder, the sin of drunkenness. But human beings are sexual in their deepest selves, and so sexual sin involves a person at his or her deepest level. The damage done by this sin strikes at the heart of what it means to be human.

Put another way, casual sex is not so much wrong as impossible and a contradiction in terms. Sexual intercourse is not casual and never can be. It is profound, for it involves opening ourselves up, even if for a brief time, in complete vulnerability to the other; it involves sharing on the deepest physical and psychological levels.

This is characteristic of human sexuality, and also what differentiates it from merely animal sexuality. Animals do not find that sexuality (or "mating," as it is usually called) involves any such psychological openness and sharing on profound levels. For them, it is simply a matter of biology and the release of the moment, and that's it. There is no possibility for profound vulnerability, for lasting commitment, for deep sharing, or for self-transcendence—in other words, for love. The spiritual component for them is entirely lacking. Sex is about procreation and nothing else.

With humanity, it is different. God invented sexuality not merely for procreation, but also for love, for enduring investment in another with whom one can find enduring security and the possibility of mutual emotional enrichment. Fornication short-circuits all this.

Nothing is automatic with us as it is with the animals. We are not forced to love or to use sex as a vehicle for love. Having made a profound and lasting unity with another through sexual intercourse, one is free to sever that connection instantly and go on to find innumerable other sexual partners. But such devaluation of sex comes at a cost, for it violates the way God made us to function.

If one severs the connection set up by sexual union, one finds it increasingly difficult to make those inner connections. If one persistently uses sex not as love's vehicle to foster lasting mutual care but only for passing pleasure, then one's inner capacity for such self-transcendence is eroded by it. One increasingly finds an inner leprosy at work within one's heart, wherein one becomes desensitized (as in the case of leprosy), worn down inwardly, and eventually deformed. A lifestyle of fornication reduces sexuality to mating, with the resultant inability to find in sex the possibility for self-transcendence and service to the other.

Sex is meant to be fundamentally unitive, to lead a person to find in another a source of joy, delight, and enrichment. Fornication devalues sex so that it becomes fundamentally not about another person but about an experience located in one's own body. True love doesn't just want the pleasure; more than anything, it wants the other person as a person. For the true lover, sex is not about a bodily experience so much as it is about one's eternal delight in the beloved.

The Internalization of Purity

In continuing to examine the "old things," the old treasures of the Law and the Prophets which continue to be valued in the new dispensation of the Gospel, we may look at our Lord's words in Matthew 5:27–28: "You have heard that it was said to those of old, 'You shall not commit adultery.' But I say to you that whoever looks at a woman to lust for her has already committed adultery with her in his heart."

In interpreting this passage, we need to place it securely in its original context. Here Christ is not legislating morality, or offering a psychological treatise on sexual temptation, or creating a systematic theology. He is warning His disciples against the approach of the Pharisees, described throughout the Sermon on the Mount (in which this passage occurs) as "the hypocrites" (6:1, 5, 16; 7:5). This teaching about inner adultery, like all the words in chapter 5 about murder, divorce, swearing oaths, retaliation, and opposing your enemies, comes under the basic heading of having more righteousness than the scribes and Pharisees (Matt. 5:20).

The Pharisees, with their self-righteous externalism, are the main target throughout this chapter and throughout the Sermon on the Mount generally. They thought our Lord too lax because He did not keep the traditions of the elders (compare Matt. 15:1–2); they thought He was minimizing the importance of the Law. Our Lord replied that, on the contrary, He did not come to abolish the Law (as they accused Him of doing), but to fulfill its original intent (Matt. 5:17). Indeed, greatness in the Kingdom of heaven would depend on keeping and teaching the command-ments of the Law (5:19). It was the Pharisees who were transgress-ing the intent and full impact of the Law with their externalism. Christ's disciples needed a righteousness greater than that of the Pharisees if they were to enter the Kingdom (5:20).

Having established this basic principle, Christ goes on to illustrate it with several examples. The first is the example of murder (Matt. 5:21f). The Law said, "You shall not murder," and the Pharisees asserted that external compliance with this com-mandment was all God required. Christ said that, on the con-trary, this commandment was not just concerned with outward murder, but with eliminating murder in the heart as well. If one cherished murderous rage within one's heart, one thereby broke this commandment. The prohibition against murder was origi-nally intended by God to seep all the way down into the inner recesses, into the inner motivations and wellsprings of action, and to soften the heart. If one were restrained from murdering one's neighbor only because one knew one would be caught and punished, this was not enough to be truly righteous. A truly righteous person would decide inwardly not to murder or cherish revengeful rage, even if he or she could get away with it.

This is how we are to understand our Lord's word about lust and adultery in Matthew 5:27f. The Law said, "You shall not commit adultery," but if one avoids adultery only because one knows one will be caught and punished, this is not enough to be truly righteous and to truly fulfill this commandment. If one "looks at a woman to lust for her"—that is, if one has already given one's inner consent to the adultery and is only dissuaded by outer unfavorable circumstances from fulfilling this desire—then one has already broken the commandment against adultery. The commandment is obeyed or broken primarily "in the heart."

Here we need to understand what is meant by "the heart," for our modern culture makes the heart the organ and locus of feeling. The phrase "I love you with all my heart" to us moderns means, "I love you with great emotional intensity." In our culture, feelings and emotions are what matter and what bestow authenticity on any action. It is otherwise in the Scriptures. There "the heart" is the locus and organ of *decision*, not feeling, of *will*, not emotion. (Emotions in biblical metaphorical anatomy are imaged by the kidneys, or "the reins"; compare Job 19:27; Ps. 16:7; Prov. 23:16.) To commit adultery in one's heart is to decide inwardly to commit adultery, to give inner consent to the act. It has little to do with feelings, provided that feelings do not produce inner decisions.

This is important, for many people interpret this word of our

Lord as condemning feelings and as saying that one is condemned if one has the psychological experience of being sexually tempted. Such temptation must be resisted, but it is not what Christ is talking about here. Christ is not saying that if one is sexually tempted by looking at a woman, one is thereby guilty of adultery. What matters to God primarily is not the feeling of being tempted, but the inner decision one makes when faced with the temptation. If one is tempted by the sight of a woman and yet resists the temptation, deciding inwardly that one would never sin with her, even if one could get away with it, then one has kept the commandment, regardless of the strength of the temptation. But if one is tempted and refuses to sin only because one knows one will be caught, then one has broken the commandment, regardless of one's outer innocence of action. In both cases, what matters is not the presence of temptation, but the inner resolution and decision.

In this word about adultery and sexual temptation, as with all the Lord's words in the Sermon on the Mount, Christ reinterprets the Law, cutting to its heart and exposing for us the Law's true and original intent. In the old days, external compliance might have been enough. But now that Christ has come, God's children must penetrate to the heart of the Law and fulfill it fully, letting God write it on their hearts.

As the prophet Jeremiah prophesied long ago, when the Kingdom would come, God would make a new covenant with His people and write His Law upon their very hearts (Jer. 31:33). This word about adultery in Matthew 5:27f and the new internalized standard required of us is part of God's new covenant provision whereby He puts His Law within the human heart. Sexual purity is now a matter of the inner heart, and our commitment to it has been radically internalized.

In these "old things" in the New Testament, we find a reinforcement of the protection given to sexuality by God in the Old Testament, providing an even more intensive bulwark against sin. God gave humanity the gift of sexuality to help us along the path of growth, raising us from the level of the animals and making something basic to our natures full of possibilities for self-transcendence. Fornication drives us from this saving path, reducing us to the level of the beasts.

The prohibitions against fornication do not witness to the evil of sex, but on the contrary to its value and preciousness. The fragile flower of possibilities for growth through sexuality needs the protection and shelter of hard prohibitions from the cold, blasting winds of this fallen world. The hardness of these counsels witnesses to the value of the gift.

The Power of Abstinence

By "abstinence" we mean the determination to deny oneself satisfaction of an appetite or desire. In our examination of the thought of St. Paul, we must distinguish this from the singleness he promotes in 1 Corinthians 7, for the two things, though related, are different.

In 1 Corinthians 7:7, Paul does express the wish that all could be given the *charisma* of continence, just as in 1 Corinthians 14:5 he expresses the wish that all the Corinthians could be given the *charisma* of speaking in tongues. In 1 Corinthians 7:25f he promotes singleness as an ideal "in view of the present distress" (probably a reference to the stressful character of the "last days," the time until the Second Coming). In verses 32-35, Paul explains more fully why he counsels single people to stay single if their circumstances permit:

> But I want you to be without care. He who is unmarried cares for the things of the Lord—how he may please the Lord. But he who is married cares about the things of the world—how he may please *his* wife. There is a difference between a wife and a virgin. The unmarried woman cares about the things of the Lord, that she may be holy both in body and in spirit. But she who is married cares about the things of the world—how she may please *her* husband. And this I say for your own profit, not that I may put a leash on you, but for what is proper, and that you may serve the Lord without distraction.

We see here that Paul's main concern in promoting singleness is securing freedom from care, the freedom to focus one's time and attention upon "the things of the Lord" and so to be "holy in body and spirit." Doubtless this pursuit of holiness included the freedom to fast and to abstain from conjugal relations, but this was not its primary component. St. Paul is not here urging singleness because it allows one to forgo sexual activity, but rather because it provides for freedom from all "worldly things"—things such as administrating a large household, managing servants, raising children, cultivating social connections, and entertaining visitors.

Paul's eye is on the less-busy schedule of the single person, not primarily on activity (or non-activity) in the bedroom. Singleness allows one more easily to simplify one's life and focus on the "one thing needful" (Luke 10:42), to engage in works of social service (the things mentioned in James 1:27), such as visiting orphans and widows in their affliction. As we examine the power of abstinence, we should not draw conclusions from Paul's words in this passage, for sexual abstinence is not here his primary concern.

Fasting from Food

Our modern and secular culture knows little of the value of fasting as the ancients understood it. For us, any denial of our bodily desires is at best unnecessary and at worst unnatural and harmful. Abstaining from food is acceptable if part of a weight-loss program, for it has an acceptable goal in mind—namely, looking slim and sexy. But abstaining from food because it is Great and Holy Friday, with the goal in mind of pleasing the Lord, is less acceptable to our culture. It may be tolerated as part of a strange and incomprehensible religion, but it will not strike a responsive chord, because our culture does not recognize pleasing the Lord as an acceptable goal in the same way as it recognizes looking slim and sexy as an acceptable goal.

This means that between the weight-loss programs in our culture and ascetic fasting in all ancient cultures, a great gulf has been fixed. The ancients would have considered the goal of looking slim and sexy frivolous and unworthy, and our present culture considers ancient fasting odd and perhaps pathological.

Nonetheless, the ancients were right about this—as all

monastics will attest. Fasting (that is, fasting from food; sexual abstinence during such fasts was assumed) brought with it inner power and the possibility of heightening one's spiritual powers and entering a higher realm. We see this in 2 Esdras.

The apocalyptic book of 2 Esdras was written in about the first century BC, with sections (chapters 1 and 2) added later by Christians in about the second century AD, and an appendix (chapters 15 and 16) added later still. In its present form, the book purports to be the revelations of Shealtiel (Gr. Salathiel), father of Zerubbabel, who was governor of postexilic Judea in the sixth century BC—also known as Ezra (2 Esdras 3:1), though Ezra lived a century later.

As an apocalyptic seer, Ezra was chosen to receive visions and revelations from the Lord. The angel Uriel appeared to him, revealing esoteric truths, but in order to learn more, he was commanded by the angel to "fast for seven days, and you shall hear yet greater things than these" (2 Esdras 5:13). This requirement of fasting to prepare oneself inwardly to enter the higher realm of revelation was repeated again and again throughout 2 Esdras—the prophet was required to fast later for another seven days (5:20), and then later for another seven days (6:35), and then yet again for another seven days (12:51). Ezra indeed received the promised visions (written down as the content of 2 Esdras), but only after fasting for a week each time.

Such a requirement seems odd to our culture. If God wants to share something with someone, why doesn't He just do it? But this did not seem odd to the ancients. They knew that man lived in a world of distraction and shadows, the eyes of his heart and mind constantly turning this way and that. In this state, he was in no shape to receive and appreciate higher and shattering truths. Our culture would view any such revelation in terms of sharing facts, information, and data—as something to be received by the mind. Not much inner preparation is required to receive delivery of such information; it would be akin to simply downloading and opening a computer file.

In fact, however, revelation from God is never simply about facts. Divine revelation fills and breaks and shatters and heals and rebuilds the heart, working like saving leaven to eventually transform one's entire life. Isaiah received a revelation from God and felt himself undone (Is. 6:5); Ezekiel received a revelation and fell on his face (Ezek. 1:28). Saul of Tarsus, though set apart from his mother's womb for his apostolic work, fell to the earth when he received a revelation on the road to Damascus and would eat or drink nothing for three days (Acts 9:4, 9). Even John the beloved disciple fell at Christ's feet as one dead when He appeared to him (Rev. 1:17). If even prophets and apostles reacted this way and found divine revelation so overwhelming, obviously men and women like us must prepare ourselves before being able to receive such things. Fasting is a part of this preparation to receive such words from God and to learn higher truths in the realm of the spirit.

Fasting is always coupled with prayer in the Scriptures. That is why it is coupled with prayer in Mark 9:29. In this passage, the disciples were faced with an extreme case of demonic possession. A boy was possessed by a terrible demon that caused him to be thrown down with grinding of teeth and foaming mouth (Mark

9:18). The father of the boy brought him to the disciples of Jesus, asking them to cast out the demon from his child in their Lord's Name, even as they had cast out demons on other occasions (compare Mark 6:13). To their amazement and chagrin, the disciples found themselves unable to cast out the demon from the child.

The Lord, of course, cast out the demon instantly. When later the disciples privately asked the Lord why they could not cast it out, He replied, "This kind can come out by nothing but prayer" (Mark 9:29). That is His reply according to the best manuscripts, such as the Vaticanus. Other manuscripts, such as Alexandrinus and Ephraemi, add the words "and fasting" to our Lord's reply. But regardless of the authenticity of the addition, we should not miss its significance—namely, that any ancient person would have assumed such prayer would be accompanied by fasting. Even if our Lord didn't specify fasting, such fasting, I suggest, would have been assumed by His hearers. The addition may not be authentically original, but it is not wrong. And it witnesses to how integral fasting was to sustained intensive prayer in the ancient mind.

Fasting was thus a fixed component in the life of the Christian from the earliest days. In His Sermon on the Mount, Christ assumed His disciples would fast, just as He assumed they would pray privately and give alms (see Matt. 6:1f, and especially vv. 16–17). After all, pious people such as the Pharisees might fast twice a week (Luke 18:12)—surely the Lord's disciples could do no less?

As long as He was with them and was invited to the homes of sinners for a banquet, the disciples would accompany their Lord to these banquets, even if they occurred on the usual Jewish fast days of Monday and Thursday. This scandalized such people as the disciples of John the Baptizer and the Pharisees (Mark 2:18), who condemned the Lord's disciples for eating on these fast days. But this was exceptional and caused by the necessity of Christ, the Physician of souls and bodies, reaching out with healing to those who were spiritually sick (Mark 2:16-17). Soon enough He would be "taken away," and after the Cross and Resurrection, the disciples would fast in those days (Mark 2:19-20).

We see this fasting in the lives of the earliest Christians reflected in the *Didache*, a church manual of sorts dating from about AD 100. Part of this composite document looks at disputed questions, such as the question of when a Christian ought to do his regular fasting. It counsels as follows: "Before baptism let the one baptizing and the one who is to be baptized fast, as well as any others who are able. Also, you must instruct the one who is to be baptized to fast for one or two days beforehand. But do not let your fasts coincide with those of the hypocrites [i.e., the Jews]. They fast on Monday and Thursday, so you must fast on Wednesday and Friday" (*Didache* 7:4—8:1). Here we see that these early Christians were encouraged to fast prior to the baptism of their new converts. All those actually involved in the baptism itself must fast, with the one being baptized fasting for "one or two days beforehand."

Furthermore, see from this passage that all Christians were expected to fast twice a week as the Jews did, though other days were chosen to differentiate the Christians from the Jews. This fast did not simply consist of abstention from certain foods, such as meat, fish, or dairy products. Rather, these twice-weekly fasts (*statio*, "station days," or "guard duty" they were sometimes called) consisted of abstention from *all* food until mid-afternoon or evening. Further, when (probably toward the end of the first century) the Eucharist was separated from its original context in the *agape* or love feast and began to be held early in the morning, the Christians would fast before coming to receive the Eucharist every Sunday. As one can see, the Church has always placed a great emphasis on the importance of fasting.

What is it about fasting, we may ask, that is so important? Why was it assumed in ancient days as preparation for receiving revelation, and why did it become an integral part of the Christian's life of discipleship? What does fasting do to a person? In a word, it makes one hungry. That seems too obvious to need stating, but we need to see how important and basic eating is to human existence to appreciate fully what the refusal to eat can accomplish. Man is, biologically speaking, primarily an eating machine.

I remember my grade ten biology teacher stating this: Man is a creature who only continues to live because he puts food into a hole near the top of his head (his mouth), lets the food pass through, and eliminates it at the other end. His feet and legs exist to carry him to his food; his hands exist to seize the food and put it into his mouth. He is, my high school teacher said, a being all of whose organs exist to help carry out these functions, a walking digestive system. Pretty much everything else in his biological existence is subordinated to the act of eating. Man could do without sex if he had to; he could do without philosophy and all cultural pursuits; but he could not do without eating.

It is not just my high school teacher who says this. Fr. Alexander Schmemann makes the same point. In his classic work *For the Life of the World*, Schmemann writes:

> In the biblical story of creation man is presented, first of all, as a hungry being, and the whole world as his food. . . . Man must eat in order to live; he must take the world into his body and transform it into himself, into flesh and blood . . . the whole world is presented as one all-embracing banquet table for man. . . . It is not accidental, therefore that the biblical story of the Fall is centered again on food.[1]

Eating is basic to our existence, not just in the sense that if we stop eating we eventually die, but also because we were constructed inwardly by God to delight in eating, to orient our lives toward this act. As Schmemann also writes, "Centuries of secularism have failed to transform eating into something strictly utilitarian. Food is still treated with reverence. A meal is still a rite—the last 'natural sacrament'."[2]

Eating is primarily what we *do*. It is in our spiritual DNA, and the most secret and deep parts of our mind, heart, and subconscious are saturated with hunger, a desire to eat. The degree to which eating is basic to our inner existence may be seen in what happens when we are unable to eat for days or weeks—in other words, when we begin to starve. The thin veneer of our civilization quickly wears away, and we will do anything to eat.

---

1 Alexander Schmemann, *For the Life of the World: Sacraments and Orthodoxy* (Crestwood, NY: St. Vladimir's Seminary Press, 1977), pp. 11, 16.

2 Ibid., p. 16.

Exactly what we are prepared to do is reflected in such biblical passages as Deuteronomy 28:52–57 and 2 Kings 18:27 (which I invite you to read). We in North America often can be heard to say, "I'm starving!" when we are quite ready to eat, but the overwhelming majority of us have never known real hunger or starvation. God grant that we never will and that the historical realities reflected in the above passages will never occur in our days. Our North American affluence and the abundance of available food hides from us the degree to which we are, in Fr. Alexander's words, "hungry beings."

Having better appreciated the true significance of food, we can now appreciate also the significance of hunger. Hunger violates or at least pushes something basic to our inner equilibrium. It threatens our existence—and therefore our self-sufficiency. David spoke of humbling his soul with fasting (Ps. 35:13), for fasting does humble the soul, pushing one's inner self to the edge, creating a spiritual void within the soul, as well as the obvious material void within the stomach. It is as we face this void and are pushed by our need toward the limits of our inner resources that we can enter a different realm.

In our normal daily life, we live superficially. Things like traffic jams, petty annoyances, and long lines bother us and often put us into a temper. We are distracted and absorbed by music, by headlines, by entertainment news. In short, we live on the surface, too easily absorbed and preoccupied by trivialities. When we fast, we have the opportunity to leave this all behind, to break through to a place where we can discern the basic from the ephemeral, what is really central to our existence from life's passing adornments.

Fasting allows us to see the world with new eyes, or at least with a renewed vision of what is essential. We see and know again in our depths that we are "hungry beings."

If we are fasting and not simply starving (that is, if our fasting is voluntary and for the sake of the Lord), we can also know again that "man shall not live by bread alone, but by every word that proceeds from the mouth of God" (Deut. 8:3; Matt. 4:4). It is because of this power in fasting that it was often coupled with prayer.

Conjugal Fasting

What has been said above regarding fasting is true in some way of conjugal fasting as well. Sex is not basic to our existence as is eating, in the sense that we can live our whole lives without sexual activity but cannot live long without food. But sexuality is basic to our lives in another way, in that we are gendered individuals regardless of whatever choices we may make regarding sexual abstinence.

As a book's title proclaimed, *Men Are from Mars, Women Are from Venus*. That is, men and women are sexual to the core in that they experience reality differently. Obviously, men and woman are overwhelmingly the same in many ways, for both, after all, are made in the image of God. But gender differentiation is not simply an anatomical matter; it shows itself in a thousand little ways as the two genders act and react to the world around them. Men and women are not interchangeable at their core (though of course they are socially interchangeable, or should be, in the job market and the voting booth). The same applies to fathers and mothers: any child knows that if one falls off a tricycle and sustains a cut or bruise, that is the time for Mommy; when danger threatens, that is a job for Dad. These gender differences witness ultimately to how basic sexuality is to our existence.

Our sexual natures and sexual appetites mean that conjugal fasting pushes us internally, just as fasting from food does. It is for this reason that Paul counsels such conjugal fasting in 1 Corinthians 7:5. As mentioned above, in his first letter to the Corinthians Paul was asked to resolve a crisis that had developed. Some said sexual activity was a fatal impediment to spiritual life and so began withholding sexual access from their spouses, quoting the (possibly Pauline) proverb, "It is good for a man not to touch a woman." Others (especially, one imagines, the other spouses affected) protested such an approach. In his response, Paul counseled the average Christian, one not especially gifted with the *charisma* of continence, to marry and engage in normal marital relations. "Do not deprive one another," he said, and then added an exception: "except with consent for a time, that you may give yourselves to fasting and prayer; and come together again so that Satan does not tempt you because of your lack of self-control."

We note here that Paul counsels occasional sexual abstinence between husband and wife, even when his main point is to urge them not to "deprive one another." The difference, of course, between this exceptional abstinence and that which they had been practicing up until then was that this exceptional abstinence was "with consent" (Gr. *ek sumphonou*, "through mutual decision"), and that it was also only "for a time" (Gr. *pros kairon*). There is no suggestion here that the normal sexual relations between spouses were wrong, or even morally ambiguous. As St. John Chrysostom said about this passage, "[Paul] does not mean that sexual relations would make the prayer unclean. He simply means that they occupy one's attention."[3] Thus the purpose of such abstinence was that "you may give yourselves to prayer."

Paul's mention of the use of such occasional times of sexual abstinence in this context highlights how powerfully such conjugal fasting aids one's prayer. Of course one may devote oneself to prayer even while remaining sexually active, but Paul here counsels times of abstinence because they make the prayer even more effective. This is because, as said above, conjugal fasting pushes one internally, just as fasting from food does. It creates a void within; it intensifies one's internal focus, allowing one access to greater spiritual resources.

Sexual congress with one's spouse is good, for it brings one closer to the spouse, binding one more deeply in a one-flesh union, helping one to transcend oneself and value the happiness of another more than one's own. Its value is in its unitive power. But though sexual union with one's spouse is good, abstaining from such union is better, for it allows both the spouses to draw closer to God. Resisting something as basic to our natures as sexuality creates an internal pressure, an empty space, which can be filled by God's Spirit. It is for this reason, no doubt, that Orthodox couples traditionally abstain from marital relations before receiving the Eucharist and during the fasting seasons of the

---

3   Homily 19 on 1 Corinthians 7.

church year. It is not because sex is wrong, but because the power that comes through fasting is better.

This power of abstinence was widely recognized in those days, even among pagans and Jews. It is a common misunderstanding that virginity was dismissed as unimportant by the pagans of that time. On the contrary, despite their sex-soaked world (or perhaps *because of* their sex-soaked world), they held that sexual abstinence was important, if not essential, to a life of higher pursuits. That life of higher pursuits was termed *philosophy*.

For us today, philosophy is a university subject, involving the mind and theories and having little to do with "real life." For us it savors only of the college classroom and is far removed from the practicalities of daily existence. It was otherwise for the ancients. Philosophy (or "the love of wisdom," which is what the word means) was an all-encompassing way of living, an approach to life that enabled one to make sense of the world around him and find fulfillment amid the hard shocks life sometimes brings. Monasticism was sometimes referred to as philosophy, as was the Christian Faith itself. And for serious philosophers, a commitment to sexual abstinence was often assumed.

It was not just among the pagans of old that such an appreciation of virginity's power could be found. Jews also knew about the power sexual fasting could bring. The second-century Galilean rabbi Pinhas ben Jair asserted that abstinence was essential to receiving prophetic wisdom and the Holy Spirit. Also, around Alexandria and elsewhere, there were groups of Jews living in community and committed to prayer, the study of the Scriptures, and celibacy. They are known to history as the Therapeutae or "healers" (or possibly "servants"; the etymology is not clear). The Jewish writer Philo, writing around the time of Christ, says that they "first of all laid down temperance as a sort of foundation for the soul to rest upon."[4]

There also existed communities of Essenes, especially in the towns and villages of Judea. Scholars debate the details of the Essene movement, and especially their connection to the Qumran community and the Dead Sea scrolls, but it appears that many of the Essene groups were pledged to celibacy. (The exclusion of women from some Essene groups seems also to have been partly motivated by the distractions women could produce, disrupting the harmony of their all-male community.)

The existence of these groups shows that Jews perceived the powerful possibilities of celibacy as did their pagan neighbors. It is hardly surprising, therefore, that St. Paul also counseled his Corinthian flock (and through them, us as well) to take advantage of the possibilities offered by sexual abstinence—even if just "for a time." Such abstinence could serve to increase the power of one's prayer.

---

4   Philo, *Ascetics III.*

Chapter 3

New Things in the New Testament

IN ADDITION TO "OLD THINGS"—teachings that can also be found in the Law and the Prophets—the New Testament contains "new things," truths not fully revealed before or at best only partially revealed. One of these concerns the nature of marriage.

The Permanence of Marriage

In our Lord's day, marriage in Israel was considered to be primarily a social contract between a man and a woman wherein they would live together, the man supporting his wife, the wife caring for the husband, and both of them rearing any children resulting from their union. This did not differ markedly from the concept of marriage in the pagan world, which also considered marriage to be a contract between a man and a woman with legal obligations binding them both. This contract could be dissolved by divorce, though customs regulating divorce differed somewhat from place to place. In Israel, there were two basic schools of thought regarding when a divorce might lawfully occur.

These schools of thought were associated with the names of two prominent rabbis, Rabbi Hillel and Rabbi Shammai. They differed over the proper interpretation of Deuteronomy 24:1-4 which allowed a man to divorce his wife because he has found "some uncleanness in her" (Deut. 24:1). The term for "some uncleanness" in Hebrew is *erwat dabar* (lit. "a shameful thing").

The rabbis differed over what this grounds for divorce referred to. Rabbi Hillel held that it referred to anything the husband found displeasing in his wife, so that he could divorce her for any reason whatsoever. Rabbi Shammai held that it referred to something morally shameful, such as adultery, and that these moral infractions therefore constituted the only legitimate reasons for a man to divorce his wife. Perhaps not surprisingly, Rabbi Hillel's more lax interpretation was the more popular view. Neither rabbi ever questioned the view that divorce was allowed, since marriage was regarded essentially as a social contract.

Christ laid down a different law for His disciples. The Pharisees once asked Him whether or not a man could divorce his wife for any reason at all (i.e., whether or not He agreed with the Pharisees in their acceptance of Rabbi Hillel's view). To everyone's surprise, Christ referred them back to the story of the original creation of man and woman wherein they became one flesh:

> "Have you not read that He who made *them* at the beginning 'made them male and female,' and said, 'For this reason a man

shall leave his father and mother and be joined to his wife, and the two shall become one flesh'? So then, they are no longer two but one flesh. Therefore what God has joined together, let not man separate." (Matt. 19:4–6)

In this passage Christ referred to the original creation stories in which God made the man and his wife "one flesh." From this Christ drew the conclusion that the man and his wife had been made one by God Himself, and that if God had thus joined them together and recreated them as a new unity, divorce was unthinkable; it constituted undoing God's work and separating what He had connected.

This was a new and previously unheard-of conclusion from the creation story and one that turned on its head the whole ancient way of regarding marriage. Jews, like everyone else back then, considered marriage as a contract, which like all contracts could be dissolved, as we have seen. Christ said instead that the permission of divorce in the Law was only a reluctant concession and not the final and full will of God. God's perfect will had been declared in the creation stories of the Mosaic Law; the later legislation of Deuteronomy 24 was allowed only because the people had hard hearts and could not bear the full weight of God's will. But now that the Messiah had come and the Kingdom was arriving, this historical concession was being revoked and God's original and perfect will again declared.

In fact, this reality whereby the husband and wife became an ontological unity of one flesh persisted despite divorce's attempts to overthrow it. Thus if a man tired of his wife and divorced her in order to marry someone else, this unity of one flesh remained.

It was not abolished simply because the husband put a piece of paper in the wife's hand and threw her out of the house. Thus "whoever divorces his wife . . . and marries another commits adultery" (Matt. 19:9). This guilt of adultery applied also to the new woman being married, since the paper legality did not obliterate the one-flesh unity their sexual union created.

This was indeed something new in Israel and in the world. Christ, basing His teaching on the story of humanity's original creation, said that marriage was more than a contract. It was a new creation, a new reality, joining two people together so deeply and profoundly that now they were inseparably joined and connected at an ontological level. Before, they were two completely autonomous persons, two separate organisms; after the sexual union of marriage, they were now a single organism: no longer two separate persons, "Adam" and "Eve," but now a new creation, "Adam-Eve." They now could not separate without doing violence to the bond that joined them together and bestowed their deepest and most lasting identity. Now they were one flesh, and legal divorce could not alter that.

That is why a divorce and subsequent marriage could be considered as adultery, since this unity remained, regardless of what society said. For two Christians married to each other and mutually committed to the path of penitence and love, divorce was out of the question; marital difficulties were to be resolved by repentance, not divorce.[5] As St. Paul would later write, "To the married I give

---

5   The pastoral ramifications of this are many and various, and should be discussed with one's priest if one feels guilt because of divorce. Here one may just say that (1) the guilt from divorce falls on the person initiating a

instructions, not I, but the Lord [i.e., in this passage we are considering], that the wife should not leave her husband" (1 Cor. 7:10).

This, of course, presupposed the marriage of a Christian to a fellow Christian. As St. Paul would later point out, Christ in His teaching did not refer to the case of a Christian being married to a non-Christian (see 1 Cor. 7:12–16). In this case, the fact that the unbelieving partner could not be counted upon to love his or her partner and avoid divorce meant that divorce became a possibility. If the unbelieving partner insisted on a divorce, the believing one should accept this and be at peace.

Christ's Word about Eunuchs

In the passage we have been considering, Matthew 19:3f, we read that Christ spoke about celibacy and eunuchs. When He spoke about the permanence of marriage, the disciples were appalled and responded, "If such is the case of the man with *his* wife, it is better not to marry." Christ replied:

> "All cannot accept this saying, but only *those* to whom it has been given: For there are eunuchs who were born thus from *their* mother's womb, and there are eunuchs who were made eunuchs by men, and there are eunuchs who have made themselves eunuchs for the kingdom of heaven's sake. He who is able to accept *it*, let him accept *it*." (Matt. 19:10–12)

In interpreting this passage, it is important to understand that it follows without a break from Christ's teaching about the

---

divorce unjustly; and (2) all guilt may be forgiven through repentance in the Church of God.

permanence of marriage. The Twelve were here thinking like mere men and therefore were appalled and alarmed at the Master's disallowance of divorce among His disciples. Christ replied, "All cannot accept this saying, but only *those* to whom it has been given." By saying this, Christ is not creating two categories of disciples— those who have been given the grace to accept His teaching and who are therefore bound by it, and other disciples to whom it has not been given and who therefore are free to disregard His teaching. Rather, He is saying that *all* His disciples are given grace and power denied to the mass of mere men; *all* of them are "those to whom it has been given."

This is what Christ says in other places as well. For example, later in this chapter He will speak about the necessity of not hoarding wealth, of giving to the poor (Matt. 19:21f). He declares that it is easier for a camel to go through the eye of a needle than for a rich man to enter the Kingdom of God (v. 24). Once again, the disciples are appalled at the high standards demanded by Christian discipleship, and they ask, "Who then can be saved?" Christ responds, "With men this is impossible, but with God all things are possible" (vv. 25–26). That is, through God's power, those following Christ can make such sacrifices and enter the Kingdom of God, passing like a camel through the eye of a needle.

Or take another example, that of John 6:41f. In this passage, many Jews heard Christ declare that He was the heavenly bread that came down from heaven, and they were scandalized at this. How could Jesus declare that He had come down from heaven? He did not come from heaven, but from Nazareth, and they knew His family well. They were shocked at this teaching and had trouble accepting it.

Jesus responded that the common person, unaided by God, could not accept this on his own. "No one can come to Me," He said, "unless the Father who sent Me draws him. . . . It is written in the prophets, 'And they shall all be taught by God' [Is. 54:13]. Therefore everyone who has heard and learned from the Father comes to Me" (John 6:44-45). Here Christ makes a distinction between the common man and a man who would become His disciple. The common man cannot accept such truth as Christ is offering. It is only when God has softened his heart, taught him, and thereby drawn him to Jesus that he can have the humility and grace to accept Christ's word.

This is the meaning of Christ's saying in Matthew 19:11. The one who had been taught by God could become Jesus' disciple and accept His word about the permanence of marriage. Such a word was too much for mere men; they would need the grace the Father gave to the disciples of Jesus to accept it. As an example of what mere men were capable of, Christ gives that of voluntarily becoming a eunuch (i.e., living in perpetual celibacy) for the sake of God's Kingdom. Some men were celibates because of congenital deficiency; some men were involuntarily castrated as slaves by other men. Such things showed all the more clearly the extraordinary nature of those who voluntarily chose celibacy for the sake of serving God—men such as John the Forerunner. If God can give such grace to men, surely He can give the disciples of Jesus the grace to accept the permanence of marriage!

The final phrase of verse 12, "He who is able to accept *it*, let him accept *it*," refers here not to the optional call of celibacy ("becoming a eunuch for the sake of the Kingdom") but, as in verse 11, to the non-optional call to accept Christian marriage as permanent.

Christ's revolutionary teaching of husband and wife being one flesh and therefore participating in a permanent unity shows the great importance of marriage. Since marriage was part of the Old Covenant (and of human culture generally), one might have expected that it would be somewhat devalued under the New Covenant. One might have expected Christ to demote the significance of marriage as He demoted the significance of ritual purity (Mark 7:1f), of the Sabbath (Mark 2:23f), and of the support of the Temple (Matt. 17:24f). Given Christ's demotion and relativization of the Jewish Law, a demotion of the significance of marriage would not be unexpected.

This makes it all the more amazing that, far from demoting the significance of marriage, Christ actually strengthened and increased its significance. Marriage was a contract under the Jewish Law, with provisions made for its dissolution. But now that the Law was giving place to its fulfillment in the Kingdom, marriage was brought forward and restored to its original and pristine ideal. In the original creation, the two were made into one flesh, and now this ideal was established as the norm for those in the Kingdom.

This meant that the Song of Solomon, with all its fierce romantic exclusivity, could once again be sung by spouses as their natural wedding hymn. Now that marriage was once again revealed to be a unity of one flesh, the spousal joy in mutual delight and sexuality could take root and blossom. The ideal celebrated in the Song of Solomon could now become a reality, for the lovers in that Song did not consider themselves as mere partners in a dissolvable marital contract, but rather as one flesh, eternally part of each other. Far from denigrating marriage and sexuality, Christ's revolutionary vision of marriage allows the spouses' bodily delight in one another to be fully celebrated. The exuberant sexuality of the Song of Solomon thus finds its natural home in the Christian understanding of marriage.

The Equality of Spouses

The teaching of Christ that husband and wife were one flesh underwent elaboration in the writings of St. Paul. With his usual acuity, he looked at the passage in Genesis that spoke of the man and his wife being made one flesh and said that this text contained a great *mysterion*—a truth hidden from the world but revealed now to the initiated, a "mystery."

The concept was a favorite one of Paul's: he refers to the gospel as "mystery" (1 Cor. 2:7; Rom. 16:25; Eph. 3:3, 9; 6:19; Col. 4:3); to the apostles as stewards of "the mysteries of God" (1 Cor. 4:1); to God's saving will in Christ as a mystery (Eph. 1:9); to the preaching of the gospel word as "the mystery which has been hidden from ages and from generations, but now has been revealed to His saints" (Col. 1:26); to "Christ in you" as "the glory of this mystery" (Col. 1:27); to Christ Himself as "the mystery of God" (Col. 2:2); to the hardening of Israel in this age as a mystery (Rom. 11:25); to the gospel plan as "the mystery of godliness" (1 Tim. 3:16).

Paul's repeated use of this term witnesses to his conviction that what they were experiencing in Christ was no sudden or accidental event, no historical "flash in the pan" or ephemeral development, but the final fruition and outworking of God's will for mankind's salvation and the goal of all of Israel's sacred history. The saving realities and power of Christ that were unfolding before their eyes had been prophesied long ages ago. Israel was the world's riddle; the gospel was the riddle's answer. And this meant that Israel's sacred literature, the Scriptures, held previously undreamt-of truths, their meaning only now revealed through Christ's coming.

Ephesians 5:
St. Paul and the Teaching of One Flesh

St. Paul's words about husbands and wives in Ephesians 5 are part of a longer section in which he exhorts all the members of the household to live together as disciples of Jesus. All Christians must "submit to one another in the fear of God" (Eph. 5:21)—that is, out of reverence for the Lord, they must serve one another in love according to their various roles. Thus he gives instructions for children and fathers (Eph. 6:1-4), for slaves and masters (6:6-9), and of course also, in the first and longest section, for wives and husbands (5:22-33). Both the wife and the husband are to relate to each other as the Church and Christ relate to each other—that is, each husband must "love his own wife as himself, and let the wife *see* that she respects *her* husband" (5:33). Men and women being different, husbands and wives have different roles.

The wife images the Church, and so as the Church follows and submits to Christ, so the wives must "submit to your own husbands, as to the Lord" (v. 22). This advice is not that surprising, especially in the ancient world, in which the subordination of wives to husbands was normal and expected. (Even then, such household advice was generally given to the husbands as the ones in charge, not to the wives. Paul here breaks with secular norms in advising the wives directly.)

But what Paul says to the husbands is more unexpected and has fewer parallels and echoes in ancient secular culture. By regarding the text in Genesis 2:24 about a man becoming one flesh with his wife as a great *mysterion* reflecting the union between Christ and His Church, Paul offers Christ as an example to the husbands of how they must relate to their wives. More precisely, just as the Church is the body of Christ as well as His bride, so the wife is the body of her husband, and therefore "husbands ought to love their own wives as their own bodies" (v. 28). Just as a man "nourishes and cherishes" his own body, so the husband must nourish and cherish his own wife. Even more than this, the husband must cherish and love his wife in the same way as Christ cherished and loved the Church (v. 25). And how did Christ love the Church? By dying for the Church, by giving Himself up for her on the cross, preferring her happiness and welfare even over His own life.

This is the measure of love St. Paul commands husbands to have for their wives. It is a daunting challenge and one that has no parallel in the secular culture of that time. Secular husbands would have expected advice about wives submitting to their husbands, but would have been astounded at the thought that this meant they must pour out their lives for their wives in return—in service and humility, even at the possible cost of pain, disgrace, and death. Christ said He had not come to be served, but to serve, and to give His life as a ransom for many (Mark 10:45). Accordingly, He knelt before His disciples to wash their feet at the evening meal and died for them and for all on the cross the next morning.

This would be astonishing enough to the ancient secular mind, which conceived of authority in terms of honor and privilege, not in terms of humility and service. It was more astonishing still for Christian husbands to be told this was also the model for them as they related to their wives. St. Paul's advice to husbands and wives, far from simply reflecting the secular norms of that time, utterly overturned them. That husbands and wives were one flesh meant that they were to imitate Christ and His Church. There was, of course, subordination in this *mysterion*, as the Church submits to her Lord and the wife submits to her husband. But there is an unexpected and radical equality in the application of this *mysterion* too, as the husband treats his wife with equality and honor, cherishing her as he does his own body and pouring out his life for her in service, as Christ did for His bride on the cross.

1 Corinthians 7:
St. Paul and the Mutual Authority of Spouses

The ontological equality of husband and wife of which Paul wrote in his epistle to the Ephesians finds expression also in his first Epistle to the Corinthians. The church in Corinth was wracked by problems—cliques, confusion over food offered to idols, confusion over spiritual gifts, doubts about the final resurrection of the flesh. It also had problems in the area of sexuality.

Some people in Corinth were apparently teaching that sex was wrong, or at least profoundly ambivalent. (As we have seen in our introduction, they would have many successors.) Accordingly, these teachers were counseling husbands and wives to abstain from marital sexual relations with each other. In some cases, the abstinence was mutually agreed upon; in other cases, there was no mutual agreement, but simply withholding of sex from one partner by the other.

The teachers counseling such abstinence thought it was all pretty simple: "*It is* good for a man not to touch a woman" (compare 1 Cor. 7:1). Indeed, wasn't Paul himself a celibate? Did not he himself value singleness and celibacy as the preferred option? (It is even possible that the aphorism "It is good for a man not to touch a woman" was a quotation—though shorn of its original context—of Paul himself; compare such [mis]uses of his own words in 1 Cor. 6:12, 13.[6])

The difficulties such a one-sided commitment to abstinence would create between married couples and in their local church community can be imagined. Word (and protest?) got back to Paul, as the parishioners appealed to him to resolve this urgent issue and give his apostolic advice. What did *he* counsel? Was it true that it was good for a man not to touch a woman and that

---

6   The Pauline words used out of their context by the Corinthians would be, "All things are lawful for me" (1 Cor. 6:12), and "Food is for the stomach and the stomach is for food" (1 Cor. 6:13)—from which the Corinthians incorrectly concluded that Paul would bless fornication.

husband and wife should therefore abstain from sexual relations

Paul's response is found in 1 Corinthians 7, and in it we see him treading carefully and delicately through his pastoral mine field. He concedes that, yes, it is true that it is good for a man not to touch a woman. But (he goes on to say), because of temptations to fornication, each man and each woman should seek a spouse. That means, he says, that the husband must "render to his wife the affection due her, and likewise also the wife to her husband." Bluntly put, they must "not deprive one another" (v. 3, 5). Celibacy is ideal, but "each one has his own gift [Gr. *charisma*] from God, one in this manner and another in that" (v. 7). That is, God sometimes gives the gift of continence, which would enable one to live in celibacy and "not to touch a woman." But this is rare, and so the mass of people who have not received this *charisma* or gift should marry.

Let us look at the passage more carefully. In verse 3 Paul writes that the husband must fulfill his duty to his wife, and likewise the wife must fulfill her duty to her husband—that is, they must not refuse each other sexual relations, as they had been doing. His rationale for this mutual fulfillment of duty is interesting and has no real parallel in the secular culture of his day. In 1 Corinthians 7:4, Paul says why the spouses may not refuse one another: "The wife does not have authority over her own body, but the husband *does*. And likewise the husband does not have authority over his own body, but the wife *does*." One might have expected Paul to ground his advice to stop depriving one another on the common-sense observation that this was creating conflict. But Paul goes deeper than such simple common sense and bases the advice on a more profound and basic ontological reality: *neither husband nor wife has authority over his or her own body*. That authority belongs to the other.

It would be hard to overestimate the revolutionary significance of this assertion. Secular pagan people (and even pious Jewish people) assumed that the husband had authority over the body of his wife. Men at least were confident that, unless they were slaves, they had authority over their own bodies. But St. Paul here denies this. He asserts boldly that the husband did not possess authority over his own flesh, his own body. Rather, his wife held the authority over his body. The same went for the body of the wife: she also did not have authority over her own body. That authority was held by the husband.

For Paul, this was one of the necessary conclusions that followed from husband and wife being one flesh. It was the real reason neither husband nor wife could legitimately deprive the other of his or her body. It is also the final outworking of Paul's demand in Ephesians 5:21 that each Christian, including husband and wife, "submit to one another." Husband and wife submit to one another in such a radical bodily way because they are one flesh. We do not see such a radical degree of mutual submission between fathers and children, or between slaves and masters, in the rest of Paul's household advice in Ephesians 5:22—6:9. Everyone has some degree of mutual submission and loving service owed their counterparts. But only in the case of spouses do we find such a radical equality and mutuality. The *mysterion* which made Christ and His Church the pattern for husband and wife turned out to have far-reaching marital consequences.

It is a commonplace in some scholarly circles (especially among those who deny the Pauline authorship of the Epistle to the Ephesians) to juxtapose the positive approach to marriage found in Ephesians 5 to the supposedly more negative and utilitarian approach found in 1 Corinthians 7. But Paul's thought on a subject as multifaceted and complex as sexuality is not well served by such simplistic dichotomies.

It is true that Paul in 1 Corinthians 7 speaks of the more practical uses of marriage, such as its being a remedy against the temptation to fornication. It is true that he advises marriage for the majority of people by way of concession for those not gifted by God with the *charisma* of continence. Paul could speak of marriage in generalities in Ephesians 5; in 1 Corinthians 7 the local situation of the Corinthians compelled him to deal with the concrete details of people's lives, with all their conflict and complexity. The pastoral necessity of such specific and detailed counseling accounts for the difference in feel between the two passages. But this difference in feel and of detail should not blind us to the essential unity between the two passages, nor to the fact that both approaches come from the same root—namely the intimate one-flesh unity between husband and wife.

In situations where marital conflict existed (with one spouse denying the other sexual access), of course Paul is compelled to write using the hard language of rights and obligations. The Greek word Paul here uses for the marital obligation is *opheile*, the same word used in Romans 13:7 to describe the debt of taxation, and cognate with the word used in the Lord's Prayer (Matt. 6:12) to describe our debts to God. When husband and wife are quarrelling like this, they need to be told in no uncertain terms that they are thereby defaulting on a debt. Such hard language is needed to quiet down shouting people.

But the rationale for the payment of the debt commanded is spelled out as the mutual ownership of the body of the other—the fact that in marriage they are still one flesh. This reality, after the hard and legal language of debts is no longer needed, can still blossom into the vision celebrated in the Song of Songs. Mutual ownership of the body of the other is the legal expression; but the same truth can also be expressed in the words, "My beloved is mine, and I am his" (Song 2:16). In 1 Corinthians 7, Paul is fulfilling their request to judge a quarrel and bring peace to a conflict. But the vision he invokes is the one-flesh unity of man and wife and their radically equal mutuality, and this can find a more lasting expression in the Song of Songs. Ultimately, Paul's vision of marriage is not about rights. It is about mutual delight.

Celibacy and the Theotokos

In the person of the Theotokos, we see the embodiment of the new power of consecrated celibacy that was breaking into the world through the gospel dispensation. She is the link between the Old Covenant and the New. Born in the time of the Law and the Prophets, through her birth-giving she became the foundation of the gospel, or (as the "Lord I Call" dogmatikon in the first tone says) "the foundation of the Faith."

Her motherhood is rooted in the traditions of the Old Covenant and forms the glorious crown and culmination of generations of "begetting" and birth-giving. Her virginity is rooted in the new-ness of the New Covenant, manifesting the possibilities of the Spirit's fullness and the age to come. But before we look more closely at her life, we must examine the linkage between the power of the Spirit in the Christian dispensation and sexual abstinence.

The Holy Spirit in the Church

The Church began with an outpouring of the Spirit on the Day of Pentecost. In the days of the Old Covenant, only a few select individuals received the Holy Spirit—prophets such as Moses (who traditionally received the Spirit at the burning bush; Ex. 3); the seventy elders called to assist him in his work (Num. 11); the other prophets, such as Isaiah and Jeremiah; and sages and kings, such as David and Solomon. The rest of Israel, though called to sanctity (the commandment said, "Be holy, for I the LORD your God *am* holy"; Lev. 19:2), did not receive the Holy Spirit in such overwhelming ways as did these special people.

Yet the prophets looked forward to "the Day of the Lord," a day when the Spirit would be poured out on *all* the people—even down to the lowest, the male and female slaves (Joel 2:29). On that day, all would have the same endowment as once was given only to prophets and kings. When the Day of the Lord came, the Spirit would be poured out upon all flesh in the land (Joel 2:28). So great would be that outpouring and that nearness to God that "whoever calls upon the Name of the Lord will be saved" (v. 32).

The Church has always proclaimed that in Jesus of Nazareth

those blessed days had arrived. He was the messianic King; He was the Lord whose invoked Name brought salvation. He was the One who received from the Father the promised Holy Spirit and poured Him out upon all His Church, even upon the lowliest, upon all who called on His Name (Acts 2:33). The Day of Pentecost was the beginning of the Day of the Lord.

In that dispensation, the Spirit was available to all in Christ's Church in a new and powerful way. Baptism was the beginning of a life lived in the fullness of the Spirit, bringing with it possibilities for access to God and for a spiritual transformation never before imagined. Things were now possible for everyone that were not possible before under the Law. In John's words, "For the law was given through Moses, *but* grace and truth came through Jesus Christ" (John 1:17). In the words of Paul, "by Him everyone who believes is justified from all things from which you could not be justified by the law of Moses" (Acts 13:39). And again: "For the law of the Spirit of life in Christ Jesus has made me free from the law of sin and death" (Rom. 8:2). This day of new possibilities meant that every disciple of Jesus could live a life of fullness by the power of the Spirit and could continually[7] "be filled with the Spirit" (Eph. 5:18).

All Christians therefore were men and women of the Spirit. They were "Pentecostals" in that all of them received the same Spirit as did the apostles on the Day of Pentecost. This Pentecostal aspect to the Church's life meant that supernatural things were now natural for the Christian. Christian life began with

---

7   The verb "be filled" in this verse is in the present tense, indicating a continual experience.

a supernatural new birth by water and the Spirit in baptism. Through the Holy Spirit given in baptismal initiation (what we today call chrismation), each believer received a spiritual *charisma* which was expected to be used in the Church for the common good. Each Sunday one received the supernatural gift of the Body and Blood of Christ in the Eucharist.

The leaders/clergy of the Church were men ordained by the laying on of hands with prayer so that the Holy Spirit would come upon them and fit them for their tasks in the Church. When one was sick, one was encouraged to resort to those leaders that they might lay on hands and pray with the anointing of oil so that the Holy Spirit would bestow healing (James 5:14f). The Church was the place of healing, of exorcism, of inspired teaching, all of which were the gifts of the Holy Spirit. Gifts of prophecy were used within the Church, and such prophecy formed the foundation of ecclesial life along with apostolicity (Eph. 2:20).

In all these things, the Church was revealed as the home and locus of the Spirit, the place where the divine gifts of forgiveness, healing, blessing, and revelation abounded, an oasis of light in a world of darkness. Within the Church, one was safe within "the kingdom of the Son of His love"; outside the Church, one was at the mercy of "the power of darkness" (Col. 1:13). Within this Kingdom, the Christian could constantly experience the power of the Spirit of God.

In today's pluralistic society, we too easily consider Christianity as one religious option among many, assuming that the alternative options to Christianity offer largely the same reality under different labels. The early Christians knew this was not true. The other religious options were delusions and half-truths; in the Church alone, as Christ's Body, one could experience liberation from the power of evil and guilt and death through the power of the Holy Spirit. In short, Christian discipleship was essentially an experience of the Holy Spirit.

Christian Abstinence and the Mother of God

Every Christian was thus called to live in the power of the Spirit; some Christians pushed that call to the maximum. From about the time of St. Anthony, these people were called monastics. All Christians lived in the Spirit, praying, reading the Scriptures, receiving the Eucharist, and fasting, and in all these ways receiving the power of the Spirit.

All people of that time, both pagans and Jews, knew that fasting from food and abstinence from sex brought special access to the world of the spirit. That is why pagan philosophers and Jewish Therapeutae and Essenes fasted from food and sex. Christians would avail themselves of such fasting and abstinence also. But because the Pentecostal Christian dispensation brought with it such undreamt-of possibilities for growth in the Holy Spirit, these monastic Christians embraced such fasting with all the greater zeal. If simple baptismal initiation offered such progress in the Holy Spirit, how much more would an entire life of unremitting abstinence, fasting, and renunciation make possible?

Thus, beginning around the time of St. Anthony in the fourth century, many Christians fled to the desert to embrace a life of celibacy, prayer, and fasting. They felt that, given the free access to the Spirit promised to every Christian, by embracing this life they could make quick and spectacular progress in the life of miraculous sanctity.

They were not mistaken. The desert soon became a city inhabited by multitudes of men and women seeking to push to the maximum the possibilities afforded by the Christian dispensation of the Spirit, though the value of such ascetic flight from marriage and the city was slow to be recognized in parts of the Church. They embraced a life of fasting, of poverty, of powerlessness, and of celibacy, all toward the goal of increasing the power of the Spirit in their life and their growth in joy.

Their hope did not prove illusory, and the desert became populated by saints, men and women whose lives were full of the Spirit's power to overcome sin, to perform miracles, and to grant revelation of the deep things of God. These monks became the athletes of God, men and women who mounted the spiritual Olympic platform to receive the gold medals of the spiritual life. And celibacy was a major part of the foundation of their life.

Christians (and pagans and Jews) in the world could testify to the value of sexual abstinence in pursuing the higher life. These monastics, under the power of the Spirit in the new Christian dispensation, could also testify to the power of that abstinence in drawing close to God and constantly living in a higher plane. As one desert Father said, "If you are willing, you can be all flame."[8]

Mary of Nazareth is the supreme example of this. In the Christian dispensation, she was the first one who was willing, who

---

8   Abba Joseph of Panephysis.

became "all flame." From the womb, she was chosen to become fire, to become the dwelling place of the Godhead. If the prophet Jeremiah was chosen from the womb for his calling as a prophet to the nations (Jer. 1:5), if St. John was chosen from the beginning for his task as the Forerunner and filled with the Spirit while still in his mother (Luke 1:15), if St. Paul was chosen and set apart for his calling as Christ's apostle from his mother's womb (Gal. 1:15), how much more would the maiden chosen to be Christ's holy Mother be set apart and prepared by the Spirit for her task from her birth?

And this preparation came to its culmination when the Holy Spirit came upon her after the Annunciation and granted her miraculous and virginal conception. It was as the archangel Gabriel said: "*The* Holy Spirit will come upon you, and the power of the Highest will overshadow you; therefore, also, that Holy One who is to be born will be called the Son of God" (Luke 1:35). From that moment onward, Mary of Nazareth became our most-holy, most-pure, and glorious Lady, the ever-virgin Mother of God. Later, many would come to be disciples of her Son and receive the Holy Spirit. Mary was the first to receive this infilling of the Spirit; she was, in a way, a Pentecostal before Pentecost.

This infusion of the Spirit meant that Mary now lived by the power of the Spirit—and this presupposed that she lived in sexual abstinence to preserve this power. Though married (and not "single" or "carefree" as Paul envisioned in 1 Cor. 7:32f), she still preserved her virginity. In Israel's sacred history, it was commonly supposed that a special infusion of the Holy Spirit brought with it the calling to abstinence. When Moses received his divine calling at the burning bush, some Jewish exegesis understood that this pledged him to future celibacy: "This Moses of flesh and blood separated himself from his wife on the day that You appeared to him in the bush."[9] It was similar with the case of the seventy elders who later received the same Spirit that God gave to Moses: when Moses' (now celibate) wife Zipporah heard that Eldad and Medad of the seventy elders received the Spirit, she cried out, "How sad for the wives of those men!"[10] because it meant they also were now pledged to celibacy.

Whether or not this was historically true in the days of Moses is not the point. The point is that this was the view of Jews in Mary's time in the first century, and Mary (and her spouse Joseph) would have considered that the infusion of the Holy Spirit she received after the Annunciation placed her in the same category as Moses and his seventy elders. That is, she now lived in the realm of the Spirit and could not diffuse His power by taking up the normal married life of sexuality. She did not choose perpetual virginity after the birth of her son Jesus because sex was evil, but because she had been chosen as a special vessel of the Spirit.

Every pagan and Jew knew that abstinence brought with it possibilities for spiritual growth. Mary (like Moses and his seventy elders before her) would now live completely and perpetually open to those possibilities. Occasional and temporary sexual abstinence would allow the one fasting access to a higher spiritual realm. Mary's perpetual virginity, to which she was called by

---

9   Cited in Max Thurian, *Mary: Mother of the Lord, Figure of the Church* (London: The Faith Press, 1963), p. 27.

10   Cited in Thurian, op. cit., p. 3.

the infusion of the Spirit after the Annunciation, meant that she would live permanently within that realm.

Mary therefore abides in the Church as an example of what the Spirit can do, living at the furthest horizon of our common destiny in the Kingdom of God. The Old Covenant was lived under the sign of Abraham, who miraculously begot Isaac through sexual union with Sarah. The New Covenant is lived under the sign of Mary, who miraculously gave birth to Jesus through a virginal conception. The Old Covenant under Abraham therefore sanctifies sexuality, and begetting, and life in this age. The New Covenant under Mary sanctifies virginity, and the Spirit's power, and the life of the age to come. Through Mary, the Old Covenant is transformed and opens out into the New Covenant, with new possibilities and access to a new spiritual power.

Summary of the Scriptural Material on Sexuality

In the Old Testament, sexuality finds its safe and unique context in marriage, considered primarily as a social and economic contract between man and woman. Though the contractual nature of marriage allows for such things as divorce and polygamy, the primordial "one flesh" nature of the marriage bond pushes the partners toward an essentially monogamous and permanent union. This is reflected in such passages as Proverbs 5:14f, which finds in the spouse a source of joy and an inspiration to fidelity, and also in such passages as the Song of Solomon, which celebrates such monogamous fidelity with fierce emotion. This elevated understanding of marriage makes adultery and fornication not simply violations of a social code that erode social stability (though they are that), but also violations of love and of the joy that God has implanted in the marriage bond itself.

This Old Testament understanding of marriage finds a home in the New Testament, as well as reinforcement. In the New Testament, Christ returns to the primordial understanding of marriage as a new creation of one flesh, and disallows things such as divorce, which were previously allowed. St. Paul mines this for its deeper conclusions, such as the essential equality of both marriage partners, as well as the permanence of the marriage.

In the New Covenant, sexuality is given a Christological context: Fornication is disallowed because it violates the prior union with Christ, for one who has united himself to Christ and holiness cannot then seek another union that would result in unholiness. Also, husband and wife mirror the eternal union between Christ and His Church, and this latter union provides the husband and wife with their mutual roles and obligations one to another. In the Old Covenant, marriage was primarily about sexuality; under the New Covenant, marriage is primarily about Christ.

The importance of sexuality forms the foundation for its transcendence in the form of consecrated celibacy. It is because sexuality, like eating, is so basic to human nature that abstaining from it can provide such spiritual power. This insight was recognized universally, by both pagans and Jews, but the new opportunities for spiritual power provided by the outpouring of the Holy Spirit upon the Church since the Day of Pentecost mean that, for the Christian, such possibilities are greatly amplified. Consequently, both married Christians and monks can experience tremendous spiritual growth as they fast from sexuality and practice abstinence. This fasting and abstinence are not based on a view that sex is evil, but rather that it is good and basic to human nature, and therefore its renunciation, either temporary (in married couples) or permanent (in monastics), can offer possibilities for spiritual growth.

Such possibilities for growth are exemplified first and best by Mary the Theotokos, whose infusion of the Spirit and consequent sexual abstinence made her preeminently a person of the Spirit, supremely advanced in holiness. Mary, the Virgin and Theotokos, revealed what could be accomplished through consecrated virginity. She is justly regarded as the patroness of monastics and the spiritual mother of all who pledge themselves to Christian chastity.[11]

---

11   The monks of Mt. Athos, for example, regard her as their patroness and
     Mount Athos as her special garden.

Chapter 4

Sexuality in the Teaching of the Fathers

THE GENTILE WORLD into which the Church moved out in the first century was a world with a rather dim view of the body. One hoped that at the end of one's life the soul could finally escape from the body and go away, perhaps to the stars, liberated at last. No wonder the pagan crowds gave Paul a hearing up until the time he suggested that after death the body would be raised again (Acts 17:32). Even several hundred years later, in the time of Augustine, the sensitive man already felt humiliated and shamed by his body.

Such attitudes could produce radically different conclusions. For some, spirituality consisted of abandoning the body as much as possible and concentrating on the soul within (this was the approach of the Manichees). Some simply decided to seize whatever bodily pleasure they could before it passed, to "eat, drink, and be merry, for tomorrow we die" (compare 1 Cor. 15:32). It was in this world that the Fathers preached the gospel and strove to find ways to interact and connect with the prevailing culture to lead men to Christ.

The Fathers and Sexuality

In speaking about the patristic approach to sexuality, great care needs to be taken. For "the Fathers" were not a small handful of men, but a multitude of writers, monks, bishops, missionaries, and preachers, working throughout the Roman world and beyond, and writing over a period of hundreds of years. They therefore exhibit all the diversity and variety we would expect from such a group. In many ways, talking about "the views of the Fathers" is a bit like talking about "the views of Western civilization," or "the views of the Americans," in that there are many voices, voices that often disagreed with one another about certain things. We can discern a certain degree of consensus, of course (which is why we can even use the phrase "the views of the Fathers"), but complete agreement in all details is hardly to be expected.

We find differences of emphasis and also disagreement about fine details (such as the famous disagreement between Ss. Augustine and Jerome about whether the quarrel between Peter and Paul in Gal. 2:11f was a genuine quarrel or a staged lesson). We find differences between East and West, and between different regions. For example, St. Augustine—and the West that looked to him increasingly for guidance—thought that if man had not fallen, sex would have been even better and more under human control than it now is; whereas in the East a consensus seemed to be emerging (influenced at least partly by Origen's work) that if man had not fallen, reproduction would not have taken place by sexual means at all, so that sex was created by God only in prescience of man's fall and mortality. One can speak of a patristic consensus, but that consensus is very broad.

The writings of the Fathers were overwhelmingly pastoral—that is, they were both occasional and contextual. By "occasional" I mean they were occasioned by situation and need. These men did not sit back in armchairs and in ivory towers and write treatises because they were bored. Rather, they responded to various needs and crises.

They preached and wrote (often upon request) to answer a heresy or false teaching threatening the spiritual health of the Church or to defend the Faith against Jewish or pagan challenge. They wrote to encourage wavering monks in their monastic commitment, to encourage married couples in their married fidelity. They wrote to rebuke worldliness in the Church, urging the faithful to courageous resistance against sinful habits that prevailed in the world. They wrote defenses of the Faith to commend it to the world.

These writings were also intensely contextual in the sense that their contents were determined by the situation they were addressing. Thus, for example, St. John Chrysostom writes a work extolling virginity. In this work, he marshals all possible arguments for remaining in virginity, such as the difficulties attending the married life. He was not addressing married people, but virgins, people who had already embraced an ascetic life of sworn chastity but who were becoming discouraged, and he must be read in this context. It would distort his thought to apply these words beyond their original purpose and context and to read him as if he were giving his final views about marriage. When he *does* address married persons (such as in his sermons), he speaks of marriage much more highly, praising it as something divine and glorious.

St. John, like the other Fathers, must be read in context if he is to be properly understood. With the notable exception of St. John of Damascus writing his *Exact Exposition of the Orthodox Faith* in the eighth century, there is hardly anything one could call "systematic theology" among the Fathers—and even the Damascene's work was very late, summing up much of what had been written before him.

In their writings and thought on sexuality, the Fathers are concerned with two basic tasks, both inherited from their reading of the Scriptures: to defend the lawfulness of marriage and sexuality, and also to promote abstinence as a way of accessing spiritual power. That is, they were fighting a battle on two fronts, combatting both those who denied the sanctity and legitimacy of sexual activity and those who scorned and disdained the new ascetic movement, which promoted abstinence. As any soldier will attest, fighting a battle on two fronts can be very difficult, but that is the task given by God to the Fathers from the culture in which they lived. This task of fighting on two separate and opposite fronts accounts for much of the variety found in the patristic writings.

The writings of the Fathers form an immense body of literature, and in a work such as this we can hardly begin to survey it. Accordingly, we will simply sample some of their works, picking out a few musical bars from a few single voices out of the vast and swelling chorus of their writings, looking at a few representatives each from the East and the West.

The Views of the Eastern Fathers

We begin in the East with our Father among the saints, John Chrysostom. The golden-mouthed preacher in his early ministry wrote in praise of consecrated celibacy—not surprisingly, since he himself once spent time in the caves of Syria practicing extreme asceticism, inspired by the hermits who lived there. Probably shortly after his return from the caves (the dating must remain imprecise), he wrote a pamphlet, *On Virginity*, referred to briefly above. In this work he extols consecrated abstinence as the most exalted way into the Kingdom, encouraging those who have chosen this path to persevere in their commitment, whatever their detractors might say.

In this treatise he writes, "Virginity is as much superior to marriage as heaven is to earth, as the angels are to men. . . . Angels neither marry nor are given in marriage; this is true of the virgin. The angels have stood continuously by God and serve Him; so does the virgin."[12] Virginity is thus a far better choice than marriage, which he describes as "a garment befitting mortals and slaves."[13] Having experienced for himself the possibilities opened up by renunciation and abstinence, John was determined that others who had committed themselves to such renunciation not be thrown off their chosen path by those criticizing their choice.

---

12   *On Virginity*, ch. 10.
13   *On Virginity*, ch. 14.

He therefore encourages these ascetics by holding out a heavenly reward for their struggle and by dismissing marriage as unworthy.

In these stark contrasts between virginity and marriage, and by his brusque dismissal of the latter, John is employing to the full his powers of rhetoric. Such rhetoric did not aim at balance or fairness; it did not weigh contrary positions and point out the differences as we moderns might do. As everyone then knew and expected, rhetoric was about arguing a case, almost like a modern lawyer. It is not the job of the prosecution to stress the extenuating circumstances that might help the defense of the one being prosecuted. The job of both prosecution and defense is to make their case one-sidedly—each assumes any needed balance will be provided by the other. It is the same with Chrysostom's defense of virginity. His aim was not to be fair to the married state, but to steel the nerves and steady the life of the person who had once chosen virginity and was now sorely tempted to abandon his or her choice because of the attractiveness of the opposite sex.

Yet St. John was no hater of marriage, and most of his flock was married. As a true and loving pastor in Antioch and Constantinople, he preached his way through the Scriptures, encouraging his people to dedicate their lives to God. Far from disdaining the married state of most of his congregation or reviling marriage as unworthy, Chrysostom exalted it, especially in one of his sermons on St. Paul's Epistle to the Ephesians. In this sermon he said:

> From the beginning God has been revealed as the fashioner of this union of man and woman, and He has spoken of the two as one. . . . There is never such intimacy between a man and a man as there is between man and wife, if they are united as they

ought to be. For truly this love is more despotic than any despotism; other desires may be strong, but this one alone never fades. For this love [Gr. *eros*] is deeply planted within our nature, which imperceptibly to ourselves attracts the bodies of men and women to each other. Do you see the close bond and connection, and how God did not allow anything from the outside to come between them? . . . Nothing so welds our lives together as the love of man and woman.[14]

Later in this same sermon, St. John gives advice to husbands and wives about how to live out this love in their marriages. As part of his advice, he says:

You ought to pray together. Both should go to church, and at home the husband should ask the wife, and the wife should ask the husband, about what was said and read there. If you should experience poverty, call to mind the holy men Paul and Peter. Remember how they spent their lives in hunger and thirst. Teach her that there is nothing in this life to fear, except offending God. If you marry in this way and with these aims you will be not much inferior to the monks; the married person will be not much less than the unmarried.[15]

In another sermon on the Book of Genesis, St. John spoke of the creation of men and women as sexual beings: "God linked [man and woman] together by their natural needs, as if by an unbroken bond when He encircled them with the chain of desire. You see how sin [at the Fall] led to woman's subjection, but how

---

14   Homily 20 on Ephesians.
15   Sermon 20 on Ephesians.

God, so ingenious and wise, used these things for our benefit."[16]

In these cited passages we see how Chrysostom believed that sexual desire was created by God to serve love and marital fidelity. Friendship between men, though deep and abiding (and such friendship, or *philia,* was valued far more highly in ancient times than in ours) could still nonetheless not compare to the power of love (*eros*) between husband and wife. That *eros* was fashioned by God as a chain of desire to bind the man and woman to each other for their mutual benefit.

Sexual desire is not stigmatized as something unfortunate or as a curse, but as God's provision and creation, "deeply planted within our nature" to do its work. That divine work is to "attract the bodies of men and women to each other." These are "natural needs," and constitute a "chain of desire." Despite our fallen state, it still represents God's "ingenious and wise" work, and is given "for our benefit."

Sexual desire can be badly misused (as John says in other sermons where he denounces such misuse), but it is part of the goodness of God's creation. Chrysostom is so optimistic about the possibilities for sanctity within marriage that he even declared that if the husband and wife were truly pious, they would "be not much inferior to the monks"—high praise from someone who wrote so effusively in praising monastic virginity.

Indeed, Chrysostom even suggests the married may have an easier time avoiding sin than the unmarried. In his treatise praising virginity, he warns the virgins:

---

16   Sermon 4 on Genesis.

The devil is not alone in harassing the unmarried. The sting of desire does this too, with greater urgency. This is clear to all, for we are not quickly overcome by the desires for things that we are able to freely enjoy, since the freedom to enjoy them allows the soul to be indifferent to them. . . . This is the first reason why there is more serenity among married people. The second is that even if at times the flame of passion struggles in them to reach a climax, sexual intercourse follows and swiftly represses it. But the virgin on the other hand has no remedy to extinguish the fire.[17]

In this passage, Chrysostom speaks of married sexuality in a way that gives one the impression it is good in itself and not tainted with sinfulness.

St. John's regard for the legitimacy of sexuality is so high that he even disallows those who would say sexual activity disqualifies one for prayer. He asks his flock, "How dare you excuse yourself from prayer after you have enjoyed the company of your own wife, although this has no blame at all? . . . Have you not heard Paul saying, 'Marriage is honorable, and the bed undefiled'?"[18] In this passage, Chrysostom seems to be saying that sexual activity the night before does not disqualify the married from receiving the Eucharist the next morning.

The Church since Chrysostom's day has developed another custom, whereby the faithful *do* abstain conjugally as a preparation for receiving the Eucharist, and this should not be set aside. Nonetheless, it is important to hear Chrysostom's voice

---

17 *On Virginity*, ch. 34.
18 Homily 51 on Matthew.

on this matter, for it witnesses to his positive view of sexuality.[1]

Chrysostom's thought regarding sexuality therefore can not be reduced to a single strand, but is multifaceted and complex, capable of application to life with all its various challenges and opportunities. He praised virginity, recognizing its spiritual power, and also lauded marriage, declaring that it also could lead husband and wife to sanctity. Both those choosing marriage and those choosing virginity were to find their champion in the golden-mouthed orator of Antioch and New Rome.

We look next at St. John's somewhat younger Eastern contemporary, St. Gregory the Theologian (known also as Gregory of Nazianzus). St. Gregory was known for his profound and poetic theology, and he was appointed bishop of Constantinople at the Council of Constantinople in 381. (He had been preaching in the capital for a short time before that, since 379. Gregory enjoyed being bishop of the worldly capital, if possible, even less than Chrysostom did, and he resigned before the end of the year, returning to Nazianzus.)

On Theophany in 381, Gregory preached a sermon on the feast. Baptisms were held the next day, and Gregory preached again, this time on the excellence of baptism. He took pains to reprove those Christians who deferred their baptism until the end of their lives (a practice common in his day). In this sermon, he exhorts everyone to hurry to baptism and not to defer it, whatever their lot in life:

---

19 I suggest that the two practices, St. John's and our modern one, deal with different issues. St. John was concerned to refute those who said that sexual activity rendered one unclean; our modern practice is based on the benefits of fasting, not on a concern with avoiding ritual uncleanness.

Are you living in virginity? Be sealed by this purification [i.e., baptism]; make this [sacrament] your life's companion. . . . Are you bound in marriage? Be bound also by the seal; make it dwell with you as a guardian of your continence. . . . Are you not yet wedded? Fear not this [baptismal] consecration; you are pure even after marriage. I will take the risk of that: I will join you in wedlock; I will dress the bride. We do not dishonor marriage because we give a higher honor to virginity. We will imitate Christ, the pure Groomsman and Bridegroom, as He both did a miracle at a wedding, and honors wedlock with His Presence. Only let marriage be pure and unmingled with filthy lusts. This only I ask: receive safety from the Gift [i.e., baptism], and give to the Gift the offering of chastity in its due season, when the fixed time of prayer comes around.[20]

In this sermon Gregory urges that baptism is for everyone, whether pledged to virginity, or already married, or single but intending to marry. For the virgin, baptism takes the place of spouse or life companion. For the married person, baptism acts to guard continence, keeping them holy and faithful within marriage. Even the single person should hasten to baptism. And here Gregory insists, in a brief digression, on the purity of marriage.

As we have seen, others in his day considered marriage to be *im*pure and therefore incompatible with Holy Baptism. Gregory insists the consecration and holiness bestowed by baptism are not eroded by marriage. He speaks boldly, "taking the risk" of pushing the homiletical boundaries of decorum; he says, "I will join you in getting you ready for marriage; I will even help dress the bride!"

---

20 *Oration on Holy Baptism*, ch. 18.

All this is to stress his assertion that marriage is honorable—for giving a higher honor to consecrated virginity does not imply, he says, that marriage is not honorable itself. In honoring marriage, he says that he is simply imitating Christ, who also honored marriage by doing a miracle in Cana of Galilee. But he has a proviso and a requirement: Marriage is pure, but only if the partners make it so and do not mingle it with "filthy lusts"—that is, with uncontrolled sexual indulgence. They must bring to their baptismal consecration the proper offering of "chastity in due season, when the fixed time of prayer comes around"—in other words, they must maintain their baptismal consecration in marriage by fasting from sex during Great Lent. Sex within marriage is "pure," but only if combined with a measure of self-control.

In our sampling of the Eastern Fathers, we come finally to St. Cyril of Jerusalem. Cyril was an approximate contemporary of St. Gregory, dying in 386, only three years before him. We have the sermons he preached to the newly baptized catechumens, who were baptized in Jerusalem on Holy Saturday in 347. In one of these sermons, he expounds "the ten points of doctrine," teaching the newly baptized about God, Christ, His Virgin Birth, His Cross, burial, Resurrection and Ascension, the Last Judgment, the Holy Spirit, the use of food and clothing, the final resurrection, baptism, and the Scriptures. He also teaches about the soul and the body.

In this teaching on the body, he talks about sexuality also. In his teaching, Cyril is concerned to defend the body against those who would disdain it as a cause of sin:

Don't tell me that the body is a cause of sin. For if the body is a cause of sin, why does not a dead body sin? Let beauties of every kind pass before a youth just dead, and no impure desire arises. Why? Because the body sins not of itself, but the soul sins through the body. The body is just an instrument, a garment of the soul, and if the soul is given over to fornication, the body becomes defiled, but if the body dwell with a holy soul, it becomes a temple of the Holy Spirit. . . . You virgins who maintain the angelic life in the world . . .—do not be puffed up against those who walk in the humbler path of marriage. For as the Apostle says, "Let marriage be held in honor among all." . . . But let those also cheer up who being married use marriage lawfully, who make marriage according to God's ordinance, and not of wantonness for the sake of unbounded license, who recognize seasons of abstinence that they may give themselves to prayer, who in our assemblies bring clean bodies as well as clean clothes into the church, who have entered upon matrimony for the procreation of children but not for indulgence.[21]

Here we see the same basic concerns as held by Cyril's contemporaries, St. John Chrysostom and St. Gregory the Theologian. That is, Cyril locates sin not in the body, as if the body were impure in itself (as the Manichees contended), but in the soul. If the soul is pure and refuses to sin (e.g., by fornication), then the body becomes a temple of the Holy Spirit. Like the other Fathers, St. Cyril holds consecrated celibates in high regard, as those living the life of angels while on earth. But he warns them not to become proud, for once again, what matters is not so much the body, with

---

21   *Lecture 4*, ch. 23–25.

its virginity, as the soul, with its humility. Virgins therefore should not boast against or disdain those who have chosen "the humbler path of marriage."

Marriage is fully acceptable to God, and one may be pure in a sexually active marriage. But, as with St. Gregory, there are some requirements. They must marry "lawfully, according to God's ordinance"—a reference not to being legally married by the state (this was assumed), but to not using marriage for the satisfaction of unbridled lust, of "wantonness" and "unbounded license." That is, instead of indulging in unrestrained sexual license, the partners must be willing to practice restraint and "recognize seasons of abstinence that they may give themselves to prayer"—that is, must refrain from sex during Lent. In this way they will bring "clean bodies" into the church for the assemblies. They would not dream of coming to church in dirty clothes; then let them be clean inside through practicing restraint, as well as outside through washing their clothes. The main point of marriage is "the procreation of children," not the "indulgence" of unbridled lust.

The Views of the Western Fathers

From the Eastern part of the Church we turn now to the West. The West in particular does not lack for negative views of sexual desire. The North African writer Tertullian sets the tone for much that is to follow. In his tract *Exhortation to Chastity* he writes to discourage men from remarrying after the death of their first wife. As his argument progresses, he asks,

What is it that takes place in all men and women to produce both marriage and fornication? Mixing the flesh, of course, the desire [Lat. *concupiscentiam*] which the Lord equated with fornication. Some one will say, "Then are you now condemning first marriages too?" Not without reason, however, for it too consists of that which is the essence of fornication.[22]

With such a low view of marriage, it is not surprising that in his tract *To His Wife,* in which he leaves her lessons to be followed after his death, he bids her not to remarry. Rather, he looks forward to their reunion in the Kingdom, where the carnal things of marriage will be no more. "There will be at that day no more resumption of voluptuous disgrace between us. No such frivolities, no such impurities."[23] Referring to sex between husband and wife as "voluptuous disgrace, frivolity, impurity" certainly reveals a fairly dim view of marriage. (It also makes us wonder what kind of relationship Tertullian had with his perhaps longsuffering wife.)

Not all shared the negativity of the hard-hitting polemicist of North Africa. But one can discern its echo in certain Western writers who followed him. In much of the secular world of that time, as we have seen, it was assumed that abstinence was fitting for a life of philosophy, and some churchmen applied this to the clergy, exalting and praising a life of abstinence. But Ambrose, Bishop of Milan from about 374, went further, taking ideas that were in the Western air[24] and acting upon them.

---

22 *Exhortation to Chastity*, ch. 9.

23 *To His Wife*, ch. 1.

24 Pope Siricius of Rome about this time wrote to Himerius of Tarragona in Spain that priests should be abstinent if they would offer the Eucharist,

Ambrose was a man deeply suspicious of bodily desires. Asexuality was the ideal for St. Ambrose, a state free from any desire. His clergy therefore, if married, must renounce sexual relations with their wives if they were to serve with him as his priests. In his book *Duties of the Clergy*, he wrote:

> You know that the ministerial office must be kept pure and unspotted [Lat. *immaculatum*], and must not be defiled by conjugal intercourse. You know this who have received the gifts of the sacred ministry, with pure bodies, and unspoilt modesty, without ever having had conjugal intercourse. I am mentioning this, because in some out of the way places, when they enter upon the ministry, or even when they become priests, they have begotten children. They defend this on the ground of old custom. . . . If the people [of the Israelites, in Ex. 19:15] were forbidden to approach the sacrifice unless they washed their clothes, do you, while foul in heart and body, dare to make supplication for others?[25]

As mentioned above, this was something new in the way Ambrose insists on it. Indeed, he even admits that those not practicing it claim they are abiding by "old custom." But St. Ambrose is uncompromising: for him, "conjugal intercourse" acts to "defile" the ministerial office, spoiling modesty and rendering "pure bodies" impure. The same thought is applied to those who are married, though not clergy. In a letter to the church of Vercellae, written around 396 on the occasion of the death of their bishop, Ambrose inveighs against lust. He writes:

"for those who are in the flesh cannot please God" [citing Rom. 8:8–9].
25 *Duties of the Clergy*, Book 1, ch. 50.

Holy Scripture teaches us that pleasure was suggested to Adam and Eve by the craft and enticements of the serpent. Since the serpent itself is pleasure and therefore the passions of pleasure are various and slippery, and as it were infected with the poison of corruptions, it is certain then that Adam, being deceived by the desire of pleasure, fell away from the commandment of God. How then can pleasures recall us to paradise, seeing that it alone deprived us of it?[26]

For Ambrose it was not pride that resulted in man's fall, but pleasure, and this suspicion of pleasure as being a "slippery" way contributes to his negative view of married sexuality. It may be reluctantly tolerated among the married laity, but not at all for his clergy.

Not all Western voices were so negative. Earlier than Ambrose, St. Lactantius, writing in North Africa in the late third and early fourth centuries, offers a more positive view of sexuality. Persecuted under the pagans, he was patronized by the Emperor Constantine and charged with education of the emperor's son Crispus. Lactantius wrote his *Divine Institutes*, refuting paganism and explaining the Christian Faith in seven books.

In Book Six he discusses the uses of the senses, such as the senses of hearing, tasting, and smelling. It is perhaps significant that he reserves his discussion of sexuality for the section on the sense of touch—that is, he is discussing actual sexual activity, and not simply tempting sights. His words are very frank and practical.[27] We quote it at some length.

26 *Letter 63*, ch. 14.
27 The editors from a more squeamish time chose to leave the passage

I come now to that pleasure which is experienced through touch which is a sense of the whole body. But I think that I should speak not about cosmetics or clothes, but only about sexual desire [Lat. *libido*]. When God had formulated the plan of the two sexes, He instilled in them the desire for each other along with delight in intercourse. He therefore mixed into the bodies of all living things a most ardent desire, so that they would rush with the greatest zeal into those affections and thereby be able to procreate. This desire appears to be sharper and more vehement in human beings, either because God wished human beings to be greater in number, or because only to human beings did God grant virtue, so that they might receive praise for controlling the pleasures and practicing abstinence. . . . Whenever *libido* brings forth these works [i.e., fornication, prostitution, and homosexuality], we must fortify ourselves against it with the greatest virtue. If someone cannot restrain these impulses, he should control them within the prescribed limit of a legitimate marriage. In this way he will attain what he eagerly desires and yet not fall into sin. For why is it that people wish to be destroyed? Certainly pleasure is a consequence of honorable works; if they seek it properly, they are permitted to enjoy right and legitimate pleasure.[28]

Lactantius in this chapter goes on to warn the married man against taking a mistress, "either slave or free," and against the sin of adultery, which he condemns equally in men and in women (something of a happy anomaly in his day). Like others of his day, he assumes that sexuality finds its natural expression and intended goal in procreation.

---

untranslated from the Latin in the Ante-Nicene Fathers collection, first published in 1886.

28   *Divine Institutes*, Book 6, ch. 23.

In Lactantius we have what is almost the opposite mirror image of Ambrose. For Lactantius, pleasure is not the cause of expulsion from paradise, but simply a part of God's provision for mankind so that they might reproduce. Sexual pleasure is not inherently wrong, and someone satisfying his sexual desires within "the prescribed limit of legitimate marriage" may "attain what he eagerly desires, and yet not fall into sin." Rather, the married couple is "permitted to enjoy right and legitimate pleasure." He also asks that they "avoid illicit desires" instilled by "our adversary," straying into fornication and other forms of sexuality forbidden to Christians. These "foreign" desires "contaminate the proper ones that are themselves sinless." In Lactantius, we find a more positive assessment of sexuality within marriage as found also in the Eastern Fathers.

No look at the Western Fathers would be complete without at least a glance toward St. Augustine, whose thought and conclusions proved to be so seminal and influential in later Western Christian civilization. St. Augustine was born at Thagaste in North Africa and eventually became priest and later bishop of the port town of Hippo Regius (meaning "Royal Port"). He spent some time as a Manichee before eventually being baptized in Milan by St. Ambrose (who, we recall, had a less than robust appreciation for sexual pleasure in marriage).

Augustine's literary output is enormous: he was always being asked to produce books, pamphlets, and tracts, and he seems never to have refused. And of course as a bishop, he was always preaching, sometimes for hours at a time. (It was more the fashion then than now.) Only the tiniest bit of his varied, developing, and complex system of thought can be examined here.

It is instructive to look first at how others looked at marriage at that time, so that Augustine's balance and moderation can be appreciated more than they usually are. It is fashionable to blame St. Augustine for everything we now detest in the medieval Western church and to demonize him as someone who was completely opposed to sex. As a matter of historical fact, his views were more moderate than those of many of his age (though not, of course, many in our own age). In his day, the ascendant ascetic movement had caused many to disdain marriage as something marginal and irrelevant to the Christian life. People thrilled to hear stories of people renouncing marriage and of married couples renouncing sex. A sensitive person in that age already felt the body to be humiliating, and sexual desire was felt to be in permanent rebellion to the faculty of reason—and that age prized reason very highly. In this atmosphere, marriage needed some "good press."

Augustine composed *On the Good of Marriage* in about 401 to be just such "good press" and to defend marriage against those who denounced it as hopelessly evil, such as the Manichees.

> The result [of Adam and Eve's joining] is the bonding of society in children, who are the one honorable fruit . . . of sexual intercourse. . . . The union of male and female is something good. . . . I do not believe that marriage is a good solely because of the procreation of children; there is also the natural association [Lat. *societas*] between the sexes. . . . In a good marriage, even if it has lasted for many years and the youthful ardor between male and female has faded, the order of charity between husband and wife still thrives. The earlier they begin to refrain from sexual

intercourse, by mutual consent, the better they will be. . . . There is an additional good in marriage, namely the fact that carnal or youthful incontinence, even the most wicked, is directed toward the honorable task of procreating children. As a result, conjugal intercourse makes something good out of the evil of lust [Lat. *libido*]. . . . To this we would add that in the very act of paying the conjugal debt, even if they demand it somewhat intemperately and incontinently, the spouses still owe to each other mutual fidelity. . . . Furthermore, even when people engage in intercourse even without the purpose of procreation, even if immoral conduct impels them to this sort of intercourse, nevertheless marriage protects them from adultery and fornication. It is not that this is *permitted* because of marriage; rather, it is *forgiven* because of marriage. . . . Conjugal intercourse for the sake of procreation carries no fault; intercourse for the sake of satisfying lust, provided that it takes place with a spouse, carries a forgivable fault [Lat. *venialis culpa*]. . . . The intercourse that is necessary for the sake of procreation is without fault, and only this belongs properly to marriage. Intercourse that goes beyond the need of procreation follows the dictates of lust [Lat. *libido*], not reason. . . . If both partners are subject to such a desire [Lat. *concupiscentia*], they are doing something that clearly does not belong to marriage.[29]

Augustine wrote this treatise before his struggle with Pelagius and the crystallization (some would say "the hardening") of his views. In about 419 he wrote another treatise, *On Marriage and Concupiscence*, in which he expounded further on the cause of sinfulness in sexuality. He writes:

---

29 *On the Good of Marriage*, I, 1; III, 3; IV, 4; VI, 6; X, 11.

It is one thing for married persons to have intercourse only for the wish to beget children, which does not have guilt [Lat. *culpam*]; it is another thing for them to desire carnal pleasure [Lat. *carnis voluptatem*] in intercourse, but with the spouse only, which has venial sin [Lat. *venialem culpam*].[30] . . . Whenever it comes to the actual process of generation, the very embrace which is lawful and honorable cannot be effected without the ardor of lust [Lat. *libidinis*]. . . . Now from this concupiscence whatever comes into being by natural birth is bound by original sin.[31]

According to this understanding, original sin (which for St. Augustine involves guilt, so "the devil hold infants guilty who are born . . . of the evil of concupiscence"[32]) is transmitted to everyone through lust, because sexual intercourse cannot be effected apart from lustful desire. This lustful desire, being evil in itself, therefore taints everyone born from it. Admittedly, Augustine defines the sinfulness of married concupiscence mildly, calling it only "venial sin," something dealt with by the normal daily repentance involved in asking for forgiveness of our trespasses in the Lord's Prayer, or by giving alms. It was reason to blush, not to feel guilty. But it still reflects a negative view of sexuality, one foreign to the thought of Lactantius in the West or of Chrysostom in the East.

Summary Reflections on the Fathers' Teaching

As we have seen, though there is a consensus among the Fathers, that consensus is very broad. All of the Fathers lived and worked

---

30   *On Marriage and Concupiscence*, ch. 17.
31   Ibid., ch. 27.
32   Ibid.

in a world in which the goodness of marriage and of sexuality was in some measure under attack. Manichees outside the Church condemned sexuality and bodily existence generally as something of a catastrophe, or at best problematic. The ascendancy of asceticism within the Church led some to devalue sexually active married Christians as "second class," pushing them to feel guilty about their sexuality or renounce it entirely, especially after the time for having children had passed. Faced with this, all the Fathers responded by defending the essential goodness of marriage and the legitimacy of married sexuality, usually quoting the apostolic declaration that "marriage *is* honorable among all, and the bed undefiled" (Heb. 13:4). Like everyone in that day of high infant mortality rates, the Fathers valued marriage as a means of procreation.

This should not be passed over lightly. In our age of mercifully lower infant mortality rates and longer life spans, an age in which we are warned often and urgently of the dangers of "overpopulation," we can forget that the ancient cities hovered on the brink of depopulation. In the second century, the average life expectancy was less than twenty-five years, with only four out of one hundred men and even fewer women surviving beyond their fiftieth birthday. It was a society worn thin by disease, famine, and war. The only defense against encroaching death and social extinction was procreation, considered a civic duty as well as a domestic joy. The fact that sexual activity usually resulted in pregnancy spoke volumes, even apart from the scriptural narrative and its command to "be fruitful and multiply" (Gen. 1:28). To say that sex was meant for procreation, for them, was to state the irrefutably obvious.

The Fathers also insisted that marriage did not exempt Christians from the challenges and task of sexual self-control, and their sermons are replete with warnings against "unbounded license." And of course married couples must avoid adultery and fornication.

The Church still called married couples to times of abstinence, even as St. Paul did in 1 Corinthians 7:5. And as well as valuing abstinence for married couples, they reserved their highest praise for the monks and virgins who made abstinence a way of life. If marriage was the silver, then such abstinence was the gold. Or, paraphrasing St. Paul's counsel in 1 Corinthians 7:38, the married person does well; the virgin or celibate does better.

Regarding the question of the essential sinfulness of married sexuality itself, it is harder to find a complete consensus. An early Western view (that of Lactantius) and the abiding Eastern one was that sexual desire itself is not wrong; it is the divinely given mechanism urging the human race to its necessary procreation. From about the time of Ambrose and Augustine, another, less positive, view was increasingly voiced in the West, which viewed sexual desire as tainted and unworthy in those aspiring to Christian holiness, especially in the clergy. This newer view saw libido as profoundly ambivalent, as something that needed further justification (such as the intended procreation of children) when indulged. The Western church increasingly insisted that its clergy be celibate, the process culminating in the twelfth century. The lack of consensus on this one point remains an abiding difference even today between the Catholic West and the Orthodox East.

In general, we may conclude that in their broad consensus the Fathers reflect the teaching of the Scriptures, upholding the goodness of marriage and promoting the possibilities offered by Christian abstinence. Because of the deep union of the husband and wife as one flesh, fornication and adultery are forbidden, as are divorce and polygamy. All Christians are called to self-control, whether married or single.

Chapter 5

The Line in the Sand

THE TEACHINGS OF INDIVIDUAL Fathers and their broad consensus find confirmation in the canons of some of the church councils. Councils were primarily pastoral affairs, convoked to solve a local (or perhaps more widespread) crisis. Most of the time it was the most prominent bishop in the area affected that called his brother bishops together to consider what to do about the problem. In the case of more widespread problems affecting the empire over great areas, it was the emperor who called together the bishops (this was the case for the First Ecumenical Council of Nicea).

In either case, it was the senior bishop who presided at the council, and he and his fellow bishops who voted, since the bishops were the local pastors of their churches. (In those days, each town or village had its own bishop.) Those at the councils commended their decisions to others for their consideration and acceptance, though of course if a bishop from elsewhere refused to accept the decisions of the council, there was little the bishops of the council

could do except break off eucharistic communion with the on_
who refused—at least until the time of Constantine, when othe_
more forcible, "remedies" became possible.

The canons passed at these councils represented the summar_
results and practical upshot of what was discussed. They were no_
so much laws as pastoral guidelines which the other bishops wer_
asked to follow. These councils and their canons are very import_
ant, for they represent more of a consensus than the work of an_
given Father or church writer, and thus have a greater claim t_
represent the wider mind of the Church.

The Canons of the Council of Gangra

Sometime in the middle of the fourth century (perhaps 340; th_
date remains uncertain), a council of bishops was held in Gangr_
under the presidency of Eusebius, probably bishop of Nicomedia_
a city with imperial connections and prominence. The purpose o_
the council was to deal with the heretical teaching and tendencie_
promoted by Bishop Eustathius of Sebaste, who was attracting
disciples throughout Armenia, Pontus, and Paphlagonia (where
the council of Gangra was held).

Eustathius is an interesting figure with a colorful history. He_
was born in about 300 in Sebaste, the capital of Armenia. His
father was bishop of the city, and he was ordained priest by him
and served among his clergy. Eustathius developed an attraction
for the new ascetic movement then arising in the Church and a corresponding contempt for what we would today call "the Establish-
ment." He accordingly went about wearing the distinctive clothes

of an ascetic philosopher, much to the distress of his father, the bishop. One imagines it was Eustathius's attitude more than his apparel that was the problem.

Anyway, his father expelled Eustathius from the church, and he moved to Egypt. At length he moved to Caesarea, where he succeeded in being ordained a priest. He drifted around a bit, traveling to Constantinople and then to his native Pontus. There he came into his own, attracting disciples to his new (some would have said outlandish) style of asceticism. Ascetic withdrawal from the world was gaining many enthusiastic admirers, and it appears that Eustathius managed to capitalize on the growing enthusiasm.

We may gain some idea of his own unique style of asceticism from looking at what the canons of the council condemn. Some care must be taken in this, however, since the canons we are examining constitute only one half of a possible conversation. It is possible some of the positions condemned did not represent the actual views of Eustathius (who may conceivably not have held all of these positions), but only the views of some of those associated with him. His movement seems to have bred radical splinter groups, such as that of his former follower Aerius, who broke away from Eustathius to form his own more extreme ascetic group.

The fact that Eustathius could be elected bishop of Sebaste in 357 after the council was held argues that he himself did not hold all the views which the council condemned. He would not have been the first person to create a movement he could not properly control. Anyway, what matters is not so much the personal views of Eustathius as the teachings that were spreading under his name and were condemned at the council.

These teachings were varied, but they all struck the common note of pride and disdain. It seems as if, under the pretext of piety and a higher spirituality, parents were abandoning their children and adult children were abandoning their aged parents, perhaps leaving them to be cared for by others so that they could pursue the "higher" life unencumbered by the needs of their dependents. Some women would leave their husbands; slaves were encouraged to run away from their "unspiritual" masters.

In addition to breaking the usual social ties and obligations, some were flaunting their spirituality with outward signs. Some refused to eat meat; some wore the *peribolaion*, the rough outward cloak of philosophers, to show their ascetic toughness and contempt of luxury, disdaining those who wore normal, more comfortable clothes. Some women would refuse to wear women's clothes, but would wear men's clothing instead and would crop their hair. These practices were motivated by the desire to show that the women were no longer subject to unspiritual husbands or fathers, but were beyond the reach of sexual distinctions.

Some people in this movement disdained the Church's liturgical customs as well. They would avoid attending the usual church services and the *agapes*/love feasts for the poor sponsored by rich Christians. They refused to attend the special feasts and vigils held for the martyrs (which admittedly could be quite rowdy; St. Augustine moved to suppress them in Hippo—much to the protestations of his flock!). Instead of attending these church events, the ascetics would meet in private homes to pray among themselves. They made a point of fasting on Sunday, when everyone else was feasting, and of not fasting when everyone else was keeping a fast. Also, they perhaps thought it scandalous that people should support the "worldly" clergy of the Church—anyway, they were not above helping themselves to some of the support that went to the clergy, taking the first-fruits usually given to the Church and encouraging people to give directly to them.

Finally, and more important to our present study, those of the Eustathian movement rejected sex as too unspiritual. This rejection doubtless lay behind the women's unisex dress and appearance, and their flight from their husbands. But the movement as a whole rejected sex as unworthy of a Christian and would counsel its followers not to sleep with their spouses. Indeed, a canon banning this abuse was the first one passed by the council: "If anyone shall condemn marriage, or abominate and condemn a woman who is a believer and devout, and sleeps with her own husband as though she could not enter the Kingdom, let him be anathema."

If the Eustathian follower was single, she (or he) would be counseled to remain single, and thus avoid the contamination of sex. These single people would make a point of denigrating any Christian who was married. Moreover, they would refuse to receive the Eucharist in church if the presiding clergyman was married. For the followers of the Eustathian movement, one could not be saved if one was sexually active within marriage. For them, the true church consisted of virgins and celibates, those untainted by sex.

All these Eustathian practices share one common element: they despise the average Christian and delight in separation and remaining aloof, all on the pretext of a superior piety and a higher, more spiritual way of life. The movement was wreaking havoc in families, churches, and society generally.

Accordingly, as said above, the local bishops of the area—thirteen bishops from Pontus, under the presidency of Bishop Eusebius—gathered in Gangra to deal with the problem. They passed twenty canons, or rules, declaring what was or was not allowed, and saying that if a person persisted in the disallowed behavior, that person was declared "anathema"—that is, barred from receiving the Eucharist in the Church until he repented. A pastoral letter accompanied the canons, addressed to the bishops (i.e., the pastors) in the affected area of Armenia, explaining the council's actions and urging the bishops to keep to the offered canonical guidelines.

In the concluding part of the letter, the bishops explained that their opposition to the ascetic practices of Eustathius did not mean they themselves were opposed to a *proper* asceticism. Rather, "we write these things not to cut off those in the Church of God who wish to practice asceticism according to the Scriptures, but to cut off those who undertake the practice of asceticism to the point of arrogance, both by exalting themselves over those who lead a simpler life, and by introducing novel ideas that are not found in the Scriptures or in the writing approved by the Church."

In writing this, the council of Gangra allowed for a true asceticism to find a place in the Church alongside the mass of average Christians who "led a simpler life," not embracing a life of abstinence. The council Fathers declared definitively that sex did not fatally taint[33] those who lawfully used it within marriage, and that those who insisted that it did had no place in the Church.

In this they were consistent with the (so-called) Apostolic Canons, which represented the venerable traditions of the Church, but which in their current form were much later than the apostolic age, dating from about the fourth century. Some of these canons condemn those who renounce marriage as if it were unclean and incompatible with sanctity and Holy Orders. For example, canon 5 reads: "Let not a bishop, presbyter or deacon put away his wife under pretense of piety; but if he put her away, let him be excommunicated; if he persists, let him be deposed." And again, canon 51: "If any bishop, presbyter, or deacon abstains from marriage, or meat, or wine, not by way of pious restraint, but as abhorring them, forgetting that God made all things very good, and that He made man male and female, and thus blaspheming the work of creation, let him be corrected, or else be deposed and cast out of the Church."

These canons reinforce the convictions held by the council of Gangra—though virginity is praiseworthy, it does not mean that marriage should be despised, and if any clergyman despises and rejects marriage as if it were incompatible with Holy Orders, he must cease.

---

33   Note the word *fatally*: the council did not address the question of whether or not sex taints *at all* those who practice it, but implicitly allowed for a diversity of opinion in this theoretical question. Lactantius would have opined, "No, it doesn't taint," and Augustine, "Yes, it does." Such nuance and theoretical questions were not considered. What *was* considered and outlawed was the extreme view that sex taints one so badly that one practicing it cannot be saved and that a Christian should not receive the Eucharist from a sexually active priest.

The Canons of the Quinisext Council

The word *quinisext* means "fifth-sixth," because it represents the canons attached to the Fifth and Sixth Ecumenical Councils held in Constantinople (held in 553 and 680 respectively), which did not produce any canons at the times they met together. This Quinisext Council was held in Constantinople in the same domed palace hall where the Sixth Council had met, and so sometimes the council is called the Council in Trullo or the Trullan Council (from the Latin *trullus*, describing the hall where they met).

The emperor of the time, Justinian II, wanted to codify a series of laws. In 692 he called a council to Constantinople to reform church law from the previous centuries and apply it to his reign throughout the Church. The makeup of the council was geographically diverse: the four Eastern patriarchs were there, along with the ambassadors of the bishop of Rome residing in Constantinople and 211 other Eastern bishops. (The Roman bishop himself was not able to be there, nor were the bishops of Ravenna and Illyricum in the West.) By the time it concluded, the council had passed a series of 102 canons.

Two Quinisext canons are of special interest to this present study. But before looking at them, we must look at certain canons passed much earlier by the African councils meeting in Carthage, because the Quinisext Council refers to the council at Carthage. These African councils were attended by St. Augustine, and we have already witnessed Augustine's insistence that his own clergy be celibate; at these Carthaginian councils, no doubt Augustine supplied a weighty voice. Not surprisingly, the Carthaginian councils and canons owe something to him and his views.

One of those Carthaginian canons reads:

> When at the past council the matter of continence and chastity
> was considered, and those three grades, bishops, presbyters, and
> deacons, so it seemed that it was becoming that sacred rulers
> and priests of God, as well as the Levites, should be continent
> altogether, by which they would be able with singleness of heart
> to ask what they sought from the Lord: so that what the apos-
> tles taught and antiquity kept, that we might also keep.[34]

In other words, clerical celibacy was now required of bishops,
priests, and deacons, for this was considered to be an apostolic
practice and to have a scriptural precedent.

Another Carthaginian canon reads, "It seems good that a
bishop, a presbyter, and a deacon, or whoever perform the sacraments, should be keepers of modesty and should abstain from
their wives."[35]

This represented the practice of the Western church in the
early fifth century, as we have seen. These canons mandate celibacy
for the major orders, so that "they would be able with singleness
of heart to ask what they sought from the Lord." The service of
supplicating God at His altar presupposed, in the minds of these
African men, the singleness of heart that came only from sexual
abstinence. These canons do not spend much time arguing their
case, for to those present it seems too obvious to require much
justification.

Another canon repeated essentially the same teaching. It

---

34   Canon 3 in the African Code.
35   Canon 4 in the African Code.

reads, "Subdeacons who wait upon the Holy Mysteries and deacons and presbyters as well as bishops should abstain from their wives."[36]

Here the canon extends the obligation of marital abstinence to subdeacons as well as deacons, presbyters, and bishops. An ancient summary of this canon reads, "should abstain even from their own wives *at the times of their ministration*"—that is, they should fast conjugally the night before they serve. The original form of the canon is less clear: it could mean, "subdeacons should contain themselves while waiting upon the Holy Mysteries" (i.e., resort to wives is allowed, but not during the times they are serving), or it could also mean "subdeacons who sometimes serve the Holy Mysteries must join the other clergy in being perpetually abstinent." Given that deacons, priests, and bishops were required in the other canons we have examined to be perpetually abstinent, it is unlikely that this present canon is to be understood as only requiring occasional abstinence when serving. Rather, complete celibacy is required of any clergy who might serve, whether subdeacons, deacons, priests, or bishops.

The Quinisext Council, meeting in 692, wanted to unify church practice the world over and could hardly ignore such Western customs, which were at variance with its own practice from apostolic times (as witnessed by the so-called Apostolic Canons alluded to above). It therefore drafted a canon of its own to deal with the matter, canon 13. It reads, in part:

36　Canon 25 in the African Code.

Since we know it to be handed down as a rule of the Roman Church that those who are deemed worthy to be advanced to the diaconate or presbyterate should promise no longer to cohabit with their wives, we, preserving the ancient rule and apostolic perfection and order, will that the lawful marriages of men who are in holy orders be firm from this time forward, by no means dissolving their union with their wives, nor depriving them of their mutual intercourse at a convenient time. Therefore, if anyone shall have been found worthy to be ordained subdeacon or deacon or presbyter, he is by no means to be prohibited from admittance to such a rank, even if he shall live with lawful wife. Nor shall it be demanded of him at the time of his ordination that he promise to abstain from lawful intercourse with his wife. . . . But we know, as they who assembled at Carthage (with a care for the honest life of the clergy) said that subdeacons and deacons and presbyters should abstain from their consorts. So what has been handed down through the apostles and preserved by ancient custom, we too likewise maintain. For it is fitting that they who assist at the divine altar should be absolutely continent when they are handling holy things.

In this canon, the Fathers of the Quinisext Council acknowledge a difference in custom between themselves and "the Roman Church," as especially expressed by "they who assembled at Carthage." They speak of this African council respectfully, saying that they assembled there "with a care for the honest life of the clergy." Nevertheless, they insist on their own Eastern practice as the one "preserving the ancient rule and apostolic perfection and order," as the one "handed down through the apostles and preserved by ancient custom." That is, they insist that presbyters and deacons and subdeacons be allowed to keep their wives after ordination and continue in lawful sexual intercourse with them—acknowledging, of course, the customary times for abstinence, such as immediately before serving at the altar: "for it is fitting that they who assist at the divine altar . . . be absolutely continent when handling holy things." In other words, sexuality within clerical marriage is allowed, even if fasting is required when serving at the altar.

It seems that the Quinisext Council interpreted the Carthaginian Council (and the practice of the Roman Church generally) as consistent with their own—that is, as only requiring "those who assist at the divine altar" to be "absolutely continent when they are handling holy things," but not necessarily at other times. Admittedly, that is one way of reading canon 25 from the African Code cited above—though it would be impossible to read canons 3 and 4 of the African Code in this way.

It is possible that the Quinisext Council thought that in so interpreting the Carthaginian canon 25, they were not imposing anything on the African Church or the West that was foreign to their own Western tradition. It is at least equally possible, I suggest, that the Quinisext Council *chose* to read the Western tradition in this manner to bring it into conformity with its own Eastern tradition. Whatever their understanding of the Western traditions regarding the celibacy of its clergy, the Quinisext Council continued in their own received path.

The papal ambassadors present during this Quinisext Council signed the document indicating their agreement with this and the other canons (for whatever reason), and the emperor and the council Fathers doubtless expected the bishop of Rome in due time would sign himself when he had the opportunity. (He did not. Eventually the matter was dropped, allowing a disciplinary pluralism to remain.)

This stand of the Quinisext Council is consistent with the local Council of Gangra held about two hundred years before it. Both allow parish clergy to remain fully married. Sexuality is not considered incompatible with sanctity or "being able with single-ness of heart to ask what they sought from the Lord."

This reinforcement of the possibility of a married parish clergy was not the only canon passed at the Quinisext Council that dealt with clergy and marriage. We look next at canon 12. It reads, in part:

> It is has come to our knowledge that in Africa and Libya and in other places the bishops of those parts do not refuse to live with their wives, even after consecration, thereby giving scandal and offense to the people. Since therefore it is our care that all things tend to the good of the flock placed in our hands, it has seemed good that henceforth nothing of the kind shall in any way occur. And we say this, not to abolish and overthrow what things were established of old by apostolic authority, but as caring for the health of the people and their advance to better things, lest the ecclesiastical state should suffer any reproach. For the apostle says, "Do not give offense to Jews, nor Greeks, nor to the Church of God" [1 Cor. 10:32].

This canon attempts to steer a pastoral path between different practices of East and West, and especially between past Eastern practice and (then) present sensibility. It acknowledges that in the past, bishops were allowed to live with their wives. But in Africa (which had a different tradition regarding celibacy, as we have seen), some of the faithful laity were scandalized by this old practice, in the (few?) places where it occurred. So, while stressing that the council respects past apostolic customs, it requires that henceforth bishops do separate from their wives. That is, subdeacons, deacons, and presbyters could continue to be married and resort to their wives, but not bishops.

Indeed, canon 48 of this council would require "the wife of him who is advanced to the episcopal dignity" to be "separated from her husband by their mutual consent and after his ordination to the episcopate enter a monastery situation at a distance from the residence of the bishop and there enjoy the bishop's provision." (What happens if said wife does *not* give her consent is not stated. Presumably the ordination of the man could not then occur.)

This would soon become the norm for the episcopate in the East, which would increasingly look to monastics to fill the episcopal office. It remains the norm for Orthodoxy to this day: only single men, either bachelors or widowers, are elected to the episcopate. (If they are not already monks, they are tonsured thus before their episcopal consecration, though the canon requires only that bishops be celibate, not monastic.)

This canon is not inconsistent with canon 13, which allowed for a married presbyter and deacon. No canon in the collection forbids marriage for clergy on the grounds that sexuality somehow taints the clergyman. Rather, the reason stated in canon 12 for the change to a celibate episcopate is the desire not to scandalize the faithful. In that day, when so many of the bishops of North Africa (the churches mentioned in the canon as being scandalized) were married and when so many celibate episcopal candidates were available, it seemed to them to be the only sensible pastoral thing to do. Of paramount importance for them was the good reputation of the Church in the world and "not giving offense to the Church of God."

This attempt to balance on the one hand freedom to marry (based on the essential goodness of marriage) and on the other hand not giving offense is reflected in another Quinisext canon also. In canon 6 we read:

> Since it is declared in the Apostolic Canons that of those who are advanced to the clergy unmarried, only readers and cantors are able to marry [Apostolic canon 26], we determine that henceforth it is not lawful for any subdeacon, deacon, or presbyter after his ordination to contract marriage. And if any of those who enter the clergy wishes to be joined to a wife in lawful marriage before he is ordained subdeacon, deacon, or presbyter, let it be done.

Reference is made to Apostolic canon 26, which allows for readers and cantors to be married, even after being made reader and cantor. This implies that the higher orders of subdeacon, deacon, and presbyter may in fact, unlike the reader and cantor, *not* marry after they have been placed in their respective orders.

Given the concern of canon 12 not to scandalize the faithful through the perceived ascetic laxity of having married bishops, it would seem that the motivation for this canon also is to avoid scandalizing the faithful through the perceived ascetic laxity of having subdeacons, deacons, and presbyters contract marriage later in life. Part of the cultural rationale underlying this canon is that marriage was felt to be useful to avoid the sin of fornication earlier in life, when the flame of desire burned more strongly. It was felt that as one became older, this flame should burn less strongly, making it easier to embrace a life of abstinence.

Thus subdeacons, deacons, and presbyters, having been married once and then widowed (or having advanced to mature age unmarried), should be able to be abstinent in their older age and not need the help of marriage. Whether or not this proved correct in every situation, this canon was concerned to avoid scandalizing the faithful, which would have happened should deacons and presbyters have married in their older age. That is, pastoral concern for the faithful of the Church proved a greater priority than the individual challenges of its clergy.

Summary of the Canonical Material: The Line in the Sand

The canons of the Council of Gangra and especially the Council in Trullo drew a line in the sand. That line separated the official position of the Church from the private opinions of this or that Father (even Fathers as prestigious as Augustine and Ambrose) and also from the more widespread opinions of churches of entire provincial regions, such as North Africa. For the African churches and the other Western churches that looked to Rome for guidance were, when all was said and done, still simply regional churches, and their views and canons did not necessarily reflect the official position of the entire Church of God as a whole, spread throughout the whole world.

That official position could only be adequately expressed, and that line accurately drawn, by the Church expressing itself through more widely representative canonical legislation. That is because each Father could express only his own views, and bishops of any given region could express only the views of their own locality. God's wisdom could be discerned when *the Church as a whole* expressed its mind—which might or might not coincide with the views of any given Father or church region. Thus more widely representative (or "ecumenical") councils spoke with more authority and with greater claim to be the true voice of the Church than did regional councils.

The decisions of the African churches (collected in the so-called African Code) represented the thought of men like Ambrose, Augustine, and Aurelian, the primate of Africa. The decisions of the Quinisext Council represented the thought of the four main patriarchs, over two hundred Eastern bishops, and the papal ambassadors in Constantinople, as well as embodying the customs and canons of antiquity stretching back to the apostles, embodied in the so-called Apostolic Canons. This latter had the far superior claim to speak for the Church as a whole and to represent its authentic voice.

That voice declared that sexuality could be combined with priesthood. The prejudices of the time might dictate that the sensitive man felt ashamed of his bodily existence. Manichees might maintain that sexuality was a tragedy for the spiritually inclined. African bishops might demand that all clergy serving at the altar renounce sexual relations as something fatal to truly effective priesthood. But the wider Church declared that, all this notwithstanding, married men living with their wives might still be priests, and the heart of the ancient customs must be upheld. Concern for the misgivings of the faithful and appreciation for the possibilities offered by abstinence would allow the Church to confine its episcopate to celibates and to require that deacons and presbyters not marry in their older age. But the goodness of marriage and sexuality was affirmed: In the apostolic Church, sex was compatible with sanctity.

Chapter 6

The Meaning of the Menaion

A NUMBER OF PEOPLE have wondered about why the Menaion, the collection of services to the saints, contained so few services to happily married Christians. Surely this indicates, they feel, that the Church believes celibacy is somehow required if one is to become holy? If not, where are all the married and sexually active people in the list of the Church's saints?

Certainly there is no denying that married sexuality is not celebrated in the Menaion and that many of its saints were celibates. Is this evidence that the Orthodox Church believes marriage is somehow unworthy, so that whatever it says in its other writings, the truth is that it has a contemptuous view of matrimony?

We begin by asking how a person ends up in the Menaion in the first place. That is, how does one qualify for inclusion in the Church's official list of saints? The answer is that this has everything to do with the grassroots enthusiasm of the laity. When all is said and done, it is the laity, the overwhelming and often silent majority of the Church, who determine who is or who is not a saint.

The Church's leadership, of course, has it prescribed role. The local synod of bishops of any given autocephalous church has the task of considering a given candidate and examining his or her life for impediments, of giving the canonical decision affirming his sanctity (i.e., "canonizing" him), of writing up his *vita* or life story, of writing the hymns glorifying him in the Church's liturgical services, of painting his icon. On the day celebrating the saint's canonization (or "glorification," to use more Orthodox language), it is the bishops who are in charge.

As said above, these leaders consider any given candidate. But here is the point: It is the mass of the laity who give any given candidate to the bishops to consider in the first place. That is, in all cases, the bishops are simply dealing with a groundswell from the faithful. Their task is to decide whether or not to put the Church's canonical and liturgical seal to something already existing in the hearts and lives of many of the faithful.

That is why informal veneration of a saint always precedes the formal and why some liturgical material and iconography often precedes the formal sentence of glorification. Such informal and advance veneration is not improper; it is customary, inevitable, and indeed essential, for how else could the bishops know whom to consider for glorification? In one sense, the official episcopal sentence of glorification simply provides the "amen" to prayer already being offered by the Church. For it is not the Church that "makes saints"; God makes saints, and the Church simply exercises its prayerful discernment to recognize what God has already done.

The question, therefore, of who is included on the list of saints boils down to this: "What does one do to come to the attention of the wider Church?" Some people seem to assume there is a centralized decision-making body with a set agenda and rationale, and that it has the responsibility to offer a certain number of saints as examples of lay holiness for married persons. The Roman Catholic examples of Luigi and Maria Beltrame Quatrocchi or of Georges and Pauline Vanier are sometimes mentioned. It is assumed here that the Church, in deciding whom to canonize, might pick out a few married laypersons to serve as examples for other married laypersons.

This is, of course, pretty much the way canonizations proceed in the Roman Catholic Church, with the centralized papacy doing most of the picking. Obviously Rome looks for some groundswell from the laity as well. But it certainly seems as if the papal process of choosing is conducted in this way—namely, from the desire to include a number of saints from this or that category, including married persons.

It is difficult to see how else people like Georges and Pauline Vanier could be included for canonical consideration (as they currently are), for though they doubtless lived exemplary Christian lives, no noticeable groundswell can be detected demanding their canonization. In their case, what seems to count is their harmonious marriage, not the already existing informal veneration of the faithful. Rome decides that it needs exemplars of the married laity's own vocation to be held out for their honor and emulation, and looking about, it finds Luigi and Maria Beltrame Quatrocchi and Georges and Pauline Vanier. This doubtless works quite efficiently in the centralized Roman Catholic Church, but historical honesty compels one to notice that canonizations took place otherwise in the early centuries—as they still do in Orthodoxy

In the early Church and in Orthodoxy today, demand for canonization arose spontaneously. That is, certain people came to the attention of the others because of something remarkable in their lives. In the early centuries, this "something remarkable" was usually martyrdom, and the Church calendar's first "saint's days" were feasts of the martyrs. Indeed, after Pascha and the Paschal cycle, the earliest layer of the Church's calendar is that of the martyrs' celebrations.

After the first age of martyrdom passed, the next remarkable things to capture the people's attention were the feats of the monastics. As the desert became a city populated with monastics pushing human limits through asceticism, people took notice. Many went to visit the monastics, and some monastics even settled in cities in a kind of urban desert. Stories were circulated about them, recording their words and celebrating their exploits. It was exciting to read of such things and to learn what Christ had done in and through these special people. Stories about monastics became ancient "best sellers," igniting the enthusiasm of average Christians and confirming for them that Christianity was indeed the true religion.

Eventually the Church's episcopal leadership embraced the new ascetic movement, and many of its bishops were former monks. Then such celibate leadership became *de rigueur*, as we have seen. All of this left its mark on the Church's official list of saints, as certain monks attracted widespread attention. Others attracted widespread lay attention also—such as famous missionaries, bishops, and pious rulers. But of course monastics predominated in claiming the admiration of the laity, since there were so many more monastics than there were missionaries, bishops, and rulers (especially pious ones).

Inclusion in the list of saints therefore began with and was rooted in popular enthusiasm. And people were enthusiastic for things that were remarkable, things that amazed and inspired them, things that showed them what was possible through the religion they themselves had embraced. They might never pay the price and practice such feats themselves, but it was still comforting and inspiring to learn that they were at least possible. And it held out promise for future possibilities—a married couple might not renounce sexuality and live together as celibates, but they would keep the idea in mind, and when one of them died, the other in old age might pursue monasticism afterward. And even when they both lived together as a married couple, the heroic example of the monks and of couples living together in celibacy would encourage them to persevere in their own humbler and temporary Lenten abstinence.

The point is that the people did not choose a saint because they felt they needed an exemplar of their own vocation. They did not spontaneously become enthusiastic for old married couples who managed to live together in pious harmony like their grandparents. Such couples might excite some minor admiration (less so then than today, with our soaring divorce rates), but not such excitement as would produce a groundswell demanding that their bishops canonize them.

Thus the comparative scarcity of happily married people in the Church's Menaion does not indicate any lack of appreciation for sexuality. Sexuality is not a barrier to sanctity. But the Menaion and the list of saints do not include all the possible examples of sanctity, only the ones that are so extraordinary and inspiring as to have come to widespread attention and have produced a ground-swell demanding episcopal attention. What counted toward canonization was something *extraordinary*, not just exemplary. A saint did not function as a representative of a category, but as an inspiration for people in all categories.

As Chrysostom said in his *Sermon 20 On Ephesians* cited above, if one marries in a certain way, one would "be not much inferior to the monks." This is true, of course, but such married persons, even having reached a sanctity not much inferior to the monks, are still nonetheless unlikely to excite a demand for canonization. People do not pour into the streets and demand the canonization of their grandparents because they lived exemplary lives, Mr. and Mrs. Vanier notwithstanding. Sanctity is *supposed* to be common in the Church (which is why we confess one *holy* Church in the Creed), and so we do not canonize everyone who achieves it. Married couples may become holy and still not become candidates for glorification as saints. Put another way, sexuality does not stop us from becoming saints (with a small "s"), but something more heroic than mere sanctity is required for us to become Saints (with a capital "S"). It is this latter heroism that is reflected in the Menaion.

In examining the actual texts of the Menaion and the words used to praise these saints, obviously we expect to find words praising the attainment of celibacy (which is something difficult), rather than words praising married sexuality (which is something normal). Take, for example, the words praising Andronicus and his wife Athanasia, whose feast day is October 9. Andronicus and Athanasia were happily married and had two children. Both of the children died when they reached twelve years old, leaving the couple understandably distraught, especially their mother Athanasia. In the emotional aftermath, the couple decided to enter the monastic life. Eventually they ended up living together in a celibate state. The texts of the Menaion praise them for such extraordinary self-control: "Putting aside the fleeting and corruptible love, and leaving it to those on earth, you bound yourselves with spiritual love, O blessed ones. Therefore you now abide in the habitations of the righteous." Some have regarded this as denigrating sexuality within marriage and wondered why this couple are included as saints when they cannot serve as an example to any normal married couple.

This is to miss the point. Those who included the couple in the Menaion and who wrote the texts praising them were not intending by this to offer them as a model for married couples, nor to comment upon the quality of married sexuality. Rather, they were intending solely to praise the couple for their extraordinary accomplishment and therefore, of course, contrasted the lasting and incorruptible quality of their love when they lived together as monastics to its previous quality when they lived together as husband and wife. The text does not suggest that there is anything wrong with married love, only that the love lived by Andronicus and Athanasia as monastics was all the more amazing. Married couples are not encouraged to imitate and reproduce their experience, but simply to be inspired by it to do whatever they can in their own lives.

It is the same with the example of St. Alexis, Man of God, commemorated on March 17. He was born in Rome to a noble family around the end of the fourth century. His parents arranged for him to marry a girl of similar Roman nobility (arranged marriages were usual in those days, and the couple might not know each other before marriage). On their wedding night, when the time came for Alexis to join his bride in the wedding chamber to consummate their marriage, he whispered a few words of farewell into her ear, returned the ring, and fled secretly, embarking on a life of consecrated virginity. The Menaion text praises Alexis with the words, "You counted your wife and fleeting wealth as but dust, desiring Christ alone who is your beloved."

Some have found Alexis's behavior appalling, as if he were abandoning his wife. Once again, this is to misread the story. One is tempted to reply to the criticism that as far as the young man Alexis was concerned, his arranged marriage, made doubtless over his youthful protests, never was his own choice to begin with, and that the young girl he left after a few whispered words was scarcely his wife in any sense worth discussing. No doubt the whole affair would have proved embarrassing to her (and probably infuriated her father, who would have felt insulted, as well as being out the money just spent on the wedding), but there is no reason to think this virginal girl would not have recovered fairly quickly and married someone else.

The ancients would have read the story not as a husband

abandoning his lawful wife, but as a young man narrowly avoid-ing a disastrous marriage for which he was never meant. What Alexis was renouncing that night was not marital responsibility, but rather status, security, and of course wealth (this last being stressed in the Menaion text). The story of his life presents his actions as something heroic and perhaps even a bit adventurous. To see in the story any misogyny is to read it askew and with thor-oughly modern eyes and agendas.

In short, we should not read the Menaion or peruse the Church's list of saints to find its attitude toward married sexu-ality. Married sexuality, with all its opportunities for love, emo-tional support, long-lasting fidelity, and stability of life, belongs to the realm of the sanctified ordinary. For the examples of the saints the Menaion offers us are examples of things that are *not* ordinary. They are *extraordinary*, and therefore alone capable of inspiring ordinary people to push on a little further toward the extraordinary themselves.

Chapter 7

The Practical Conclusions

IN THE INTRODUCTION TO THIS WORK, we noted the world has often gained the impression that the Church is too negative about sex. In response, we have looked more deeply at our traditions to see what the Church's teaching on this matter actually looks like. We examined the Scriptures, looking at the foundational teaching of the Old Testament, and have seen that it presents sexuality and marriage as a gift from God. We have seen this confirmed in the New Testament, which also contains new teachings about the essential equality of husband and wife, as well as new possibilities for spiritual growth in the practice of abstinence when inspired by the Holy Spirit.

We examined some of the multifaceted teachings of the Fathers in all their variety, both in the Eastern and Western parts of the one Church. We have looked at the canonical traditions of some of the church councils and seen how the broad consensus of the Fathers finds expression in some of its canons. We have had a quick look at the Menaion, since some people have used its hymnography to allege that the Church's praises of the saints are inconsistent with its patristic, liturgical, and canonical teaching, and that it represents a more negative view of sexuality.

To briefly answer our initial inquiry about whether the Church is too negative about sex, we say: No, the Church is not too negative about sex. Rather, the present world, with its obsession with casual sex, is not well placed to understand the Church's teaching about the power of abstinence.

At the end of these examinations, what are the practical conclusions? How should the average Christian grapple with sexuality? The answers may be arranged under four headings and given in the form of four assertions, each with its separate set of implications.

1. Sexuality is a gift from God, deeply ingrained in our natures, given to serve mutual love. From this assertion come three implications.

First of all, fornication violates the basic purpose of sex, for it isolates physical sexuality from any real relationship of love. Our culture refers to this severance as "casual sex" and celebrates it in a multitude of books, novels, magazines, movies, television shows, and entertainment news. Many, if not most, so-called romantic comedies take casual sex for granted as normal.

In this secular portrayal of casual sex, sexual unions are rarely if ever encumbered by unwanted pregnancy, venereal disease, or one-sided emotional attachments and heartbreak. That is, the secular portrayal of casual sex is based on a series of lies, for unless one has eroded one's authentic humanity and reduced sexual activity to mere animal mating, casual sex is not possible between human beings. All sexual encounters deeply involve the two partners.

As said above, sex unites two people on the emotional level as well as the physical, leading each person to find in his or her partner a source of joy, delight, and enrichment. All fornication militates against the formation of this inner bond, so that sex becomes fundamentally not about another person, but about an experience located in one's own body. For this reason alone, Christians must flee fornication as something incompatible with discipleship to Jesus and even with basic human integrity.

Secondly, Christians who are engaged to be married must wait until the marriage has taken place before having sex with each other. Once again, this runs counter to our prevailing culture, which assumes premarital cohabitation, sometimes even on the part of Christians. Especially after the two are engaged, the thought is, "Why wait? We're going to be married soon anyway—why abstain until then?"

The rationale for abstaining until the marriage ceremony is rooted in the significance of the ceremony itself—namely that in the ceremony, a gift is given. For a Christian, the essence of the marriage ceremony is not in its legality or in the fact that the couple is then "pronounced man and wife," but in its sacramentality, in the liturgical moment when each is given to the other by God.

Our eucharistic life in the Church trains us to receive life and joy as gifts: we do not rush in and take them for ourselves, but wait until the proper moment when someone else gives them to us. In the Divine Liturgy, for example, the communicants do not rush to the altar, take the chalice from the Holy Table, and help themselves on the rationale that they will be allowed to receive it eventually. Rather, they wait patiently until the Gifts are brought out, and then they receive at the hand of another, namely the priest. Waiting is the essential component in grateful sacramental receiving. Protesting with the words, "I'm going to be receiving Holy Communion soon anyway, so why not rush in and help myself now," would show a certain insensitivity to the holiness of the Gift.

It is the same with waiting until marriage before having sex. The gift of one to the other is given by God through the prayers of the Church; one must wait until God gives each partner to the other. To have sex before that time would be like a communicant helping himself to the Chalice. Appreciation of the magnitude of the gift given in marriage demands that one wait until it is given. Otherwise one severs the physical aspect of sex from love, which is exactly the problem with fornication.

Thirdly, sexuality in marriage is meant to unite the married couple in an ever-deepening emotional bond, so that each sexual act contributes to their mutual attachment and commitment—in other words, to love. Helped and inspired by the pleasure sex brings, each partner stays with the other in mutual service, fidelity, and kindness. These fruits of fidelity, kindness, and the ever-strengthened emotional bond remain and grow stronger even into old age, when the ardor of sexual desire has faded. Thus sex is not simply for the pleasure of the moment but serves to unite the couple in an emotional bond that will outlast the pleasure.

It is taken for granted, of course, that the option of divorce is excluded from the outset for the disciples of Jesus. Each married partner serves the other for the Lord's sake. Their fidelity to one another is the result of their mutual obedience to Christ: He forbids them to divorce, and so divorce is out of the question. Having discounted divorce as an option at the outset, the couple find they must resolve their conflicts and work things through, since Christ requires them to stay together and to love one another.

Such obedience has its reward, even in this life. A marriage in which the partners will stay together only for as long as one makes the other happy ("for as long as we both shall love," as one silly Hollywood wedding vow phrased it) is a house built on sand. For there will come times when your partner will *not* make you happy—as you do not always make your partner happy. A marriage built solely on beauty or on the joys of sex is built on false hopes, for eventually everyone will lose the outer beauty and fall prey to wrinkles, sickness, and old age. A marriage built on obedience to Christ—a marriage in which both partners forge an ever-stronger emotional bond through lifelong mutual service—such a marriage will survive the ravages of time and old age.

Thus sexuality in marriage is meant to serve love and to bring the partners ever closer to each other until they end their lives in Christ. In other words, it is meant to provide a path to the Kingdom.

2. Sexuality is meant for procreation. This assertion also has several implications.

First of all, recognizing that sexuality is meant for procreation means recognizing homosexual marriage as a contradiction in terms. In the world, gay marriage is increasingly accepted as an alternative to "traditional marriage," the marriage between man and woman. In this secular world, marriage is considered to be the institutional legitimization of feelings of love, and if two men or two women share feelings of love for one another, why should they be denied their institutional legitimization in marriage?

It is a good question. The answer, of course, is that marriage is *not* simply the institutional legitimization of feelings of love between two people, but the institutional joining of two people for the ultimate purpose of procreation. Sometimes, due to health problems, such procreation is not possible, but that does not in itself alter the basic purpose of marriage; for given normal health, repeated sexual union eventually results in pregnancy and offspring.

Since homosexual unions and activity cannot by definition result in this end, such unions cannot be defined as "marriage." Society may or may not decide to grant certain legal privileges to such unions, but the granting of such privileges does nothing to alter the definition of marriage as humanity has defined it from the beginning. Such a (heterosexual) definition of marriage is not the exclusive preserve of Christians. Everyone has always held to such a definition of marriage, be they Christian, Jewish, pagan, or Zoroastrian. The current devotion to political correctness cannot ultimately change such a venerable custom. Marriage is by definition heterosexual, whatever our current political correctness might dictate.

Gay marriage now finds a prominent place in the ongoing culture war raging within our society. Given this war, it becomes necessary to speak very precisely about homosexuality in general and gay marriage in particular. Specifically, it must be stressed that God does not hate the homosexual or anyone else. God loves the homosexual, just as He loves everyone, for His love for His creatures does not cease when they behave sinfully. And because God loves the homosexual, we must love him (or her) also. The homosexual is still our neighbor, and Christians are commanded to love their neighbors, regardless of sexual orientation and regardless of their behavior.

Of course, this love is compatible with a call to repentance. We may love the homosexual and still call for repentance from homosexual behavior, just as we may love any other sinner and still call for repentance from their sin. But angry denunciations and expressions of hate are forbidden to us and do nothing to add persuasiveness to our calls for repentance. The subject of homosexuality is a large one, and cannot be dealt with here.[37] Suffice it to say that our personal rejection of homosexual practice and non-support for gay marriage should come from a heart of love.

Our current culture of contraception has done much to instill a basic hostility to the idea that marriage is meant for procreation. This culture has in fact sundered repeated sexual activity from its usual inevitable result of procreation, so that sex (i.e., sexual pleasure) is now considered an end in itself. Sex now has little to do with having babies, so that if a man's casual sexual partner becomes pregnant, he is surprised.

---

37 A good book dealing in greater detail with the subject is Thomas Hopko's *Christian Faith and Same-Sex Attraction* (Conciliar Press, 2006).

This surprise illustrates how far our secular culture has strayed from the insights and instincts of prior ages. In previous centuries stretching back to time immemorial, sex was inextricably linked with procreation, and this linkage was a source of joy for all. Homosexual unions can gain support for the idea that they are also "marriages" only because our culture has already sundered the idea and purpose of marriage from procreation. But this essential purpose remains nonetheless.

The repeated sexual unions between husband and wife are primarily meant to unite them in an emotional bond of love, but they are also meant to result in children, and the children represent the tangible and physical evidence of this love. By loving each other in mutual self-sacrifice, husband and wife find that they have grown, changed, been transformed, and that the whole they have jointly built is more than the sum of the two parts. Proof of this is the child that is born from this love, for the child is more than either of them, being built physically and literally from both of them. The fact that the child shares DNA from both parents witnesses to the true unity of the child's father and mother and proves that love creates something true and enduring—for the child will endure when both father and mother have gone. None of this can result from the sexuality of gay couples, and this means that gay sexuality cannot fulfill the purposes of God.

Secondly, to say that sexuality is meant for procreation means that the parents must devote themselves with the all resources available to them to nurturing their children. In our culture, this usually involves limiting the size of one's family to ensure that those resources are adequate to care for and nurture all the children. In other words, it often involves the use of birth control.

In the days and culture of the Fathers, the Christian use of birth control was unthinkable: cities always seemed to hover on the brink of disaster, and whole populations felt themselves threatened with extinction. As mentioned above, in the second century, the average person lived less than twenty-five years (factoring in high rates of infant mortality), with only four out of one hundred men and even fewer women surviving into their fifties. Given this situation, most couples wanted as many children as possible, and as soon as possible, and birth control made no sense. Indeed, having a large family was considered to be a civic duty.

The Fathers therefore had much to say in denouncing the use of birth control—and the use of abortion. In their time, people who used birth control often resorted to abortion also, and for the same reason—not to limit the size of their families or to space out the births of their children, but rather to eliminate children from the marriage altogether. Such an approach to marriage was not open to Christians.

But the situation has changed from the days of the Fathers. Infant mortality rates have dramatically fallen, health care has made tremendous strides, and average life spans have therefore vastly increased. The populations of cities of North America now no longer feel under threat. All this means that the patristic lack of enthusiasm for birth control needs to be reinterpreted for a completely new situation. In the old days, producing a baby every year was only good sense, for this ensured that two or three children at least would live a full life span. Now producing a baby every year would be economically catastrophic for the average North American, for almost certainly all of them would live their full life span.

I suggest therefore that a Christian couple may legitimately use some form of contraceptive, assuming of course that it is a true contraceptive—that is, that it prevents conception and not just implantation of the fertilized egg within the womb. (The couple may want to consult a doctor to confirm that the form of birth control they are considering is not abortifacient, producing abortions.) Orthodox Christians believe that human life begins at conception, so that children within the womb are still adorned with the image of God.

It is allowable to use such contraceptives to plan, space out, and limit the size of one's family—though not to eliminate the possibility of children altogether, for as we have said, procreation is one of the main purposes of marriage. It is because of this that birth control is allowed: one may justly limit one's family size in order to have the necessary resources to nurture the children one has.

The legitimacy of the use of birth control, I suggest, is not affected by whether the kind of birth control used is "natural" or "artificial." Indeed, the very terms "natural" and "artificial" are themselves rather artificial, for both today involve the use of some degree of scientific knowledge and technology. What matters ultimately is the parents' determination to bring to the children they have created all the resources of money, time, and love they can offer.

3. Sexual abstinence offers possibilities for spiritual growth.

This conclusion brings with it two or three implications.

Firstly, affirming that sexual abstinence can aid spiritual growth in Christ means embracing such abstinence as part of the life of Christian discipleship. Just as husband and wife fast from food during Great Lent and the other seasonal fasts, and also fast from food as part of their preparation to receive the Eucharist, so they also should fast conjugally. Details of this fasting discipline vary from place to place, but basically the couple is called to abstain conjugally the night before receiving the Eucharist (e.g., Saturday night, in preparation for the Sunday morning Eucharist) and during the fasting days of the year. Such conjugal fasting does not indicate that sex is bad any more than fasting from food would suggest that food is bad. In both cases, it is because what is fasted from is good and basic to our natures that the abstinence has value. Differences in details of local practice and other personal challenges may be resolved by consulting one's parish priest.

Such fasting should not be approached legalistically or mechanically, any more than prayer or other spiritual disciplines should be approached legalistically or mechanically. When it becomes a normal and habitual part of our life, it is possible to treat it this way and not to give it much thought. But one's fasting will be more fruitful if intentionally and deliberately offered to God, asking Him to fill the void with the power of His Spirit. The aim of fasting, as with all spiritual discipline, is to gain spiritual fruit and draw closer to God; the fast should be undertaken in this spirit and with this expectation.

Secondly, a single person (or perhaps an older widowed person) should not rule out the possibility of embracing perpetual abstinence in the form of monasticism. As St. Paul says in 1 Corinthians 7:7, this ideal state can be embraced only if God has given the *charisma* of self-control. If He seems not to have given this gift, then a single person should look to marriage as the most sensible option.

In this matter, it is not the case that there is a goal, an ideal, a golden standard, to which everyone should aspire. Some have thought God has two ways of life from which all may choose: the best (monasticism) and a lesser one (marriage). They have thought God really calls all to reach for the highest way of life and become monastics, but if one cannot, then He will be reluctantly satisfied if one can only reach the lower way of life and choose marriage. That is, we should all reach for the gold medal, but most of us will have to be content with the silver medal. In this thought, marriage is distinctly second best, God's lesser will for those not strong enough to fulfill His perfect will, which is monasticism.

This is not the thought of St. Paul. For him, what mattered supremely was the individual call of God, which differs for every person. As he wrote to the Corinthians later in the same epistle, God gives different gifts, tasks, and callings to different people, to each person a different gift and calling, according to His will (1 Cor. 12:4–11). Each gift is valuable in itself, and one should not be disappointed if one receives a different gift than another person receives, nor should one devalue the gift one has actually been given (v. 15). What matters is not which gift God has decided to give to a person, but rather that person's faithfulness in using it well.

Thus, God does not give the *charisma* of celibacy (1 Cor. 7:7) to everyone, but only to some. It is these who should consider becoming monks, not those to whom God has not given that *charisma*. Those who have not received this *charisma* should consider that God has not called them to monasticism, but that God's perfect will *for them* is in marriage. They will receive the "gold medal" on the Last Day if they use the married state to serve their spouse and family. What matters ultimately is not which state we choose for ourselves, but discerning God's calling for our own lives and being faithful in that.

A further word may be added regarding single persons who have not deliberately chosen to remain single and who would like to marry, but who remain single nonetheless. It seems the contemporary Orthodox Church in North America could do a better job of recognizing and caring for these single Christians than it is currently doing. It is not the case that everyone who is not married is therefore called to become monastic; and anyway, such opportunities to embrace true monasticism and live in a monastery are hard to find in North America.

Such a person, while remaining open to the possibility of marriage, should accept that singleness seems to be God's will, at least for now, and use that singleness to draw close to Him. Continence will not be easy, yet God will give the necessary grace and strength to maintain chastity even in this difficult time of waiting. The God who fed His people with manna while they sojourned in the desert and who brought water from the rock when no other water was available will not abandon the single person while he or she sojourns in his or her own desert. The loneliness can be a great desert indeed. But it can also provide the solitude in which to find God and to grow, and it is on these opportunities that the single person should focus, not on the painful absence of a life partner.

4. Sexuality is temporary and confined to this age.

Finally, we must remember that sexuality, with all its joys, challenges, and sorrows, is confined to life in this age. In the age to come, sexual expression—the "marrying and giving in marriage" (Matt. 22:30)—will be no more. Sexuality and gender are gifts written into our bodily existence at creation; our life in this age is a gendered existence, characterized by both procreation and death. In the age to come, a new order will prevail. After the resurrection, both of these twin realities of procreation and death will be done away, and our bodily existence will transcend them, whatever will be the nature of our resurrection bodies.

As St. Paul said, in this age our life is that of Adam, the first man "from the earth," and we are "earthy" like him (Gen. 2:7; 1 Cor. 15:47). That is, we partake of all the attributes of a merely earthly and earthbound existence—we need to eat in order to live; we live by labor, "by the sweat of our face" (Gen. 3:19); we survive as a race only through procreation; and we return finally to the earth from which we were first taken.

But as we were created from the man from the earth, so we were recreated in baptism from the man from heaven, Jesus Christ, and will share the final fruits of His victory over death when we also are raised from the dead and inherit the age to come. As He is "heavenly," so also will we be (1 Cor. 15:48), and one day we will share all the attributes of His heavenly existence: we will no longer need to labor, and eat, and weep, and die. And we will no longer need procreation, for death (which procreation alone held at bay for us as a race) will be abolished. The full and glorious details of what the life of the age to come will be like have not been revealed to us. All we know is then we "will be like the angels in heaven," who neither marry nor are given in marriage (Matt. 22:30).

Because we are unable to comprehend all the glory and joy that will come flooding into our bodies and lives in the age to come, some have secretly lamented the absence of marriage in that age. For them, the absence of sexuality seems to entail a withered, ghostlike, unbodily existence, or else a bodily existence in which one is eternally fasting, and neither of these two envisioned possibilities sounds very appealing. The truth is that the joy that will flood us in that day will be so overwhelming as to make married sexuality pale and weak by comparison, and transcending it will not be felt as a loss. As C. S. Lewis said in writing about this difficult-to-imagine future life, it might better be described as "trans-sexual" than "sexless."[38]

Lewis here sounds a much-needed note. With all the many

---

38 C. S. Lewis, *Miracles* (London: HarperCollins, 2002), p. 261. (We note in passing that Lewis's use of the term "trans-sexual" predates our contemporary use of the term and that he means something quite different by it.)

joys and challenges with which our sexuality presents us in this life, we must not forget the joys of the life to come. Sometimes we can take sex too seriously. Certainly our current culture takes it too seriously, even to the point of obsession. We should take sex seriously as we take all God's gifts seriously—that is, with gratitude and determination to use it well, as He intended. But we must remember that the center of our existence is not here, but on the adoration of God.

Praise, thanksgiving (Gr. *eucharistia*), this is the true center of our existence. In our Sunday worship and in our private and family prayers, we make praise and adoration our central task, for this task and privilege will remain ours in the age to come. In that age, any labor or arduousness in fulfilling the task of praise will vanish, and praise will become as effortless as breathing. The joy in prayer we now experience only in fleeting glimpses will then be our overwhelming and constant companion.

In describing that life for which we hope, we may close with the words with which St. Augustine closed his major work, *The City of God*:

> There we shall be still and see; we shall see and we shall love; we shall love and we shall praise. Behold what will be in the end without end! For what is our end but to reach that Kingdom which has no end? To that end and that Kingdom may the good Lord bring us all.

About the Author

Archpriest Lawrence Farley currently pastors St. Herman of Alaska Orthodox Church (OCA) in Langley, B.C., Canada. He received his BA from Trinity College, Toronto, and his MDiv from Wycliffe College, Toronto. A former Anglican priest, he converted to Orthodoxy in 1985 and studied for two years at St. Tikhon's Orthodox Seminary in Pennsylvania. He has also published the multivolume *Orthodox Bible Study Companion Series* as well as *The Christian Old Testament: Looking at the Hebrew Scriptures through Christian Eyes; Let Us Attend: A Journey Through the Orthodox Divine Liturgy; Following Egeria: A Visit to the Holy Land through Time and Space; The Empty Throne: Reflections on the History and Future of the Orthodox Episcopacy;* and *Unquenchable Fire: The Traditional Teaching About Hell.*

To purchase other books by Lawrence R. Farley, please visit store.ancientfaith.com.

Ancient Faith Publishing hopes you have enjoyed and benefited from this book. The proceeds from the sales of our books only partially cover the costs of operating our nonprofit ministry—which includes both the work of **Ancient Faith Publishing** and the work of **Ancient Faith Radio**. Your financial support makes it possible to continue this ministry both in print and online. Donations are tax-deductible and can be made at **www.ancientfaith.com.**

 **ANCIENT FAITH RADIO**

Bringing you Orthodox Christian music, readings, prayers, teaching and podcasts 24 hours a day since 2004 at **www.ancientfaith.com**

CPSIA information can be obtained
at www.ICGtesting.com
Printed in the USA
FSHW010737160320

9 781936 270668